P9-DNU-364

Brunswick County Library
109 W. Moore Street
Southport NC 28461

WITHDRAWN

HAM BISCUITS,
HOSTESS GOWNS,
and
Other Southern Specialties

ALSO BY JULIA REED

The House on First Street:
My New Orleans Story

Queen of the Turtle Derby
and Other Southern Phenomena

HICKMANS

HAM BISCUITS, HOSTESS GOWNS, and Other Southern Specialties

AN ENTERTAINING LIFE (WITH RECIPES)

● ● ●

JULIA REED

ST. MARTIN'S PRESS ▨ NEW YORK

Brunswick County Library
109 W. Moore Street
Southport NC 28461

HAM BISCUITS, HOSTESS GOWNS, AND OTHER SOUTHERN SPECIALTIES. Copyright © 2008 by Julia Reed. All rights reserved. Printed in the United States of America. For information, address St. Martin's Press, 175 Fifth Avenue, New York, N.Y. 10010.

www.stmartins.com

Library of Congress Cataloging-in-Publication Data

Reed, Julia.
    Ham biscuits, hostess gowns, and other Southern specialties : an entertaining life (with recipes) / Julia Reed.—1st ed.
        p. cm.
    ISBN-13: 978-0-312-35956-0
    ISBN-10: 0-312-35956-X
    1. Cookery, American—Southern style. 2. Entertaining. 3. Southern States—Social life and customs. I. Title.
    TX715.2.S68R44   2008
    641.5975—dc22

                                                          2008005314

First Edition: July 2008

10 9 8 7 6 5 4 3 2 1

For my mother,
the best hostess I know

contents

II ❀ CHEFS I'VE KNOWN

introduction

everal years ago, in my former apartment in Manhattan, I threw a going-away party for my close friend and editor Michael Boodro, who was leaving *Vogue* to become editor-in-chief of *Garden Design* magazine. It was spring, and in honor of the occasion I was mindful that a horticultural theme should be more or less in play. But in the end, except for covering a cake with brightly colored flowers, I did what I always do for big parties. I passed silver trays of ham biscuits (hot buttered Marshall's biscuits with a thin slice of ham, country or otherwise, tucked inside), along with pimento cheese sandwiches (on Pepperidge Farm Very Thin wheat, cut into strips), watercress sandwiches (rolled, with sprigs sticking out of one end), and cucumber sandwiches (on rounds of regular Pepperidge Farm white with homemade mayonnaise). On the dining table there were: platters piled with crabmeat maison (jumbo lump crabmeat mixed with homemade mayonnaise, capers, and thinly sliced scallions) accompanied by toast points; steamed asparagus spears with bright yellow curry dip; deviled eggs (I use my friend Rick Ellis's recipe, which boasts both butter and mayonnaise); and thickish slices of rare beef tenderloin with horseradish sauce and Sister Schubert's yeast rolls. Sometimes I substitute lamb or pork for the beef (and a chutney mayonnaise for the horseradish sauce), and occasionally I will also add a platter of smoked salmon with brown bread and dill butter. I can't remember if I did the latter for this particular gathering; what I do know is that people went crazy.

Now at this point I had lived in New York for more than a decade. My own friends were used to the transplanted Southern specialties I always had on offer, but this group was mostly made up of Michael's friends, and they had clearly never dipped an asparagus spear into a bowl of curry dip or bitten into a hot ham biscuit in their lives. In a city where "hors d'oeuvres" all too often mean ubiquitous skewers of dried-out chicken saté or half-cooked snow peas with an ambiguous "fish paste" piped inside, it is relatively easy to wow people, and I have yet to discover a deviled egg or a giant lump of crabmeat bathed in homemade mayonnaise that didn't do the trick. What I didn't expect was the call I got the next day from a guest who was then an editor at the *New York Times Magazine*. "How would you like to write about food?"

So it was that the essays and recipes collected in this book came into being. To this day, I feel (almost) guilty for having been paid for them, such was the pleasure I derived in putting them together.

I am a person whose bedside reading is almost always a stack of cookbooks; my most fervent hope is that some really smart, very rich person will buy the once-great New Orleans creole palace Antoine's and give me total control over the place. Such is my obsession with this particular dream—and just in case it ever comes true—I regularly drive my husband crazy sounding out ideas for the daily specials I plan to offer in the restaurant's underused front room, where I also intend to install a marble-topped oyster bar. There is nothing that makes me happier than discovering a new canapé or spending long days—and nights—planning a party. I have clocked so many hours with my friend Keith Meacham, who, like me, was born in the Mississippi Delta, armed with legal pads and Post-it notes, poring over seating charts and mapping out possible menus, that her husband Jon, the author and editor of *Newsweek*, now refers to us—with more than a hint of derision—as the "crabmeat caucus." (In spite of himself, he appreciates what we're up to—he inaugurated *Newsweek*'s first-ever food column, after all, and generously asked me to pen it.)

This obsession with food and entertaining is not my fault. I grew up in a place where restaurants were few and cooking was of paramount importance. We give food away as presents and peace offerings, and sometimes just because it is so incredibly good that we have no choice but to share it. (One of my favorite utterances is an emphatic, "You have just *got* to taste this.") We tote it to people in times of grief (when my grandparents were killed in a car wreck, the first thing my mother told me to do as she ran out the door was to empty the refrigerator); we use it to say bon voyage or welcome back. I was never home from boarding school for more than ten minutes, for example, before a family friend named John Gannon would appear at the back door with a pot of the red beans and rice he knew I'd been deprived of; when I finally got married, his widow gave me his recipe, beautifully written in calligraphy on a now-spattered card.

Giving a party was as natural as breathing, and almost as necessary and frequent (there wasn't a lot else to do, but the people were really interesting). The party for Michael was an example of what my mother will only refer to as a cocktail supper, a term I tried for years to introduce to New Yorkers without much success. Essentially, a cocktail supper is an event that is for all practical purposes a cocktail party (a lot of people, a lot of booze) but one with enough food to constitute supper should you care to avail yourself of it, which also means it does not come to a screeching halt at eight P.M. It is not called a buffet supper because in addition to the fact that the word "buffet" is somehow slightly tacky, it does not include dinner plates or even silverware, both of which would interfere with your ability to hold and imbibe a cocktail. Every item is designed to be eaten fairly easily and neatly with your hands, and the most you can hope for is a small plate or, in my house, stacks of cocktail napkins with which to wipe your fingers. It is one of my favorite kinds of parties to give, as well as one of my favorites to attend, because my progress—talking, laughing, drinking, meeting people, quickly escaping them should the need arise—is not hindered by the task of getting a plate and finding a seat. This is also true of a cocktail party, but the food on hand at a cocktail supper is far more substantial than the odd passed canapé, so that your progress is also unhindered by falling down drunk. But in Manhattan, where people often endeavor to pack multiple events into their evenings, I found that they were confused. If they had a dinner date or another cocktail engagement to attend, they usually regretted it—they thought they were locked into a sit-down supper and thus could not risk stopping by.

Such was not the case at home. The cocktail supper remains such a staple that I feel sure that by now my mother has thrown at least a thousand of them—along with brunches and luncheons and formal sit-down dinners, not to mention catfish fries, poolside picnics, and dances in our backyard. But she is hardly alone and, best of all, every generation was allowed to get in on the act. When I was five years old, my mother and her best friend Bossy McGee gave an Easter dinner party for me and for Bossy's two daughters, my friends Anne (whom I refer to as "McGee" in life and on these pages) and Elizabeth. There is a photo of the event in which I am wearing a pale yellow dress with a handmade lace collar and white Mary Janes, sitting with five other girls and boys at one of the two formally set round tables on our terrace at home in Greenville. The tables were lit by beautifully striped, egg-shaped votive candles that Bossy and Mama had spent days making by pouring layers of pastel-colored wax into hollowed-out eggshells. The candlelight lent a magical element to the proceedings, and we all were thrilled by the solid chocolate eggs they made by pouring melted Hershey bars into still more hollowed out eggshells.

I still cannot fathom what possessed them to go to such elaborate—and elegant—lengths for our young selves, but in the years since, I have seen them devote the same amount of attention to countless other shindigs, including the rehearsal dinner given for Bossy's nephew and his fiancé, for which they made homemade chicken Kiev for more than a hundred people, pounding and rolling countless chicken breasts around pats of cold herbed butter. No task was ever too much to take on. When I was eleven and we had just begun dismantling our house for a major renovation, my father, typically oblivious to such details, announced that a famous author, who was also a political columnist and magazine editor, was flying into town for dinner in three days' time. Immediately, doorframes were remounted, a fireman who moonlighted as a painter came every morning at two A.M. to paint over what damage had already been done. Forty people were quickly invited by phone and, due to the number, it was decided tables would be set up inside and out. My mother bought a raft of old wicker chairs for the outdoor seating, so she and Bossy and various other friends and neighbors set about making seat cushions, armed with staple guns and bolts of pale green cotton canvas.

It was a landmark event of sorts because my mother planned

what would become her legendary standby, the short-notice-but-elegant menu Bossy dubbed the "V.D. Dinner," referring to the various "visiting dignitaries" who would partake of it over the years. Though by now it has endured variations driven by my mother's occasional whims and changing seasons, the basics remain pretty much the same: rare tenderloin or a rib-eye roast, butter lettuce with avocado and pink grapefruit, wild rice pilaf, spinach and artichoke casserole, scalloped oysters, homemade yeast rolls, and either charlotte Russe or chocolate mousse for dessert.

By the time the writer arrived, no one could tell the house had been in utter disarray just a few days earlier. One of our friends, a totally charming ex-patriot Brit cotton farmer, was also a vibraphonist, so he brought his vibes just in case the spirit moved the writer, who was a gifted pianist. The spirit moved both of them—a lot—and I remember that Bossy's very good-looking niece danced on the table to at least one number, and that I went to sleep listening to the writer's rousing version of "Cielito Lindo" which in those days I knew only as the "Frito Bandito" song. When the writer's wife, an accomplished Manhattan hostess, returned home, she wrote my mother for the oyster recipe.

I loved the excitement that went into those kinds of triumphs, and from a very early age I tried to produce a few of my own. Since my mother insured that my own birthday parties were the stuff of legend (every year, from the time I was two until he retired, they were written up by local newspaper columnist Brodie Crump), I insisted on planning the birthday parties of my mother and father, choosing the menu and the guests, and setting at each place the same crepe paper surprise balls that I enjoyed at my own celebrations. Again, it is astonishing to me that my parents and their friends so enthusiastically indulged me in these endeavors, but they did, and I owe whatever confidence I have as a hostess to the fact that those early efforts were not shot down, or worse, laughed at.

Somewhere along the way I also learned to cook. I was fascinated by my mother's *Mastering the Art of French Cooking,* one of the few cookbooks she owned that was bound like an actual book, rather than with the usual plastic binders of various Junior League publications. By the time I was ten, I had made so many quiche lorraines that my Uncle Mike, my Aunt Frances's beloved second husband whose fine gift-and-antiques store featured a cooking school in the basement, gave me an enormous porcelain quiche dish with a lovely horn-handled server, both of which I still have. From our family cook, Lottie Martin, I learned the importance of the cook's hand. Lottie could follow and excel at any written recipe my mother gave her, but when she made things like mashed potatoes or biscuits or even pie crusts, I noticed that she never followed a single instruction—and that her versions were always far better than anyone else's.

Lottie died way too young—I was fourteen—but my mother had cooked alongside her for enough hours to have absorbed many of her tricks, and when I went off to college I dutifully copied many of Mama's "greatest hits" in a bound blank book that I still refer to all the time. None of our undergraduate friends knew what to make of the parties my roommate and I gave in our Georgetown apartment, since the usual college fare of blocks of cheese and canned dip was replaced by a slightly more economical version of the menu for the party in honor of Michael. Instead of studying my Logic textbook, I planned elaborate brunches featuring Craig Claiborne's cheese grits, my mother's curried fruit, and slow-scrambled eggs with braised artichoke bottoms and mushrooms from the battered volume of *Mastering the Art* I had claimed as my own. When I reached my twenties, other then-revolutionary cookbooks joined it on my shelf: Alice Waters's *Chez Panisse Menu Cookbook, The Silver Palate Cookbook,* and Wolfgang Puck's first outing, *Modern French Cooking.* On a visit home, I made a birthday dinner for my father from the latter—shrimp in a mustard tarragon sauce and carrot loaf, both recipes I still use—but the California chardonnays we were all just learning about replaced the surprise balls.

These days I own hundreds of cookbooks, and many august cooks whom I mention on these pages have served as influences, but when I entertain I almost always return to the fare of my youth, the stuff my mother and Bossy and countless numbers of their friends put on their tables: fried chicken and tomato aspic with dollops of homemade mayonnaise, country ham with homemade hot mustard, fried oysters and pickled shrimp and hot crabmeat mormay, seafood gumbos and stews, curried rice salad and squash casserole, salted pecans and peppery cheese straws. The list, thank God, is endless because, like my mother, I throw a lot of parties. But the driving theory behind each offering is the same. As Mama once asked me when I was headed down a particularly fraught and too-ambitious dinner party path: "Why don't you just serve something that tastes really good?" This is not as easy as it sounds. It requires a certain sense of security for one thing—there are still a lot of people in this world who are convinced that a snow pea piped with an indiscernible pink paste is chicer than, say, a humble ham biscuit; that deviled eggs are for picnics only, that a French roll from a fine bakery is more impressive than a yeast roll cooked in an aluminum pan. They are wrong of course, and it is a lesson I am profoundly grateful that I learned at an early age.

PART I
EATING THE SOUTH

Miss Congealiality

❖

Several years ago my mother had a four-day house party during which she served an almost exclusively gelatin-based menu. I don't think it was on purpose; she just wanted to make everything in advance so she could spend as much time as possible with her friends. But by the end of the second day, when the guests had already consumed a crabmeat mousse, a strawberry mousse, two kinds of tomato aspic, and a charlotte russe, one complained that he could not get up from the table. "I think," he said, "my blood has coagulated."

None of the rest of us saw anything funny about the food. This was in the Mississippi Delta, after all, where congealed items are a staple of our diets. In *Gourmet of the Delta*, a cookbook put together by the region's Episcopal churchwomen, there are seventy salad recipes, and fifty-one of them contain gelatin; in *The Memphis Cook Book*, twenty-three of the thirty-three salads are congealed. I didn't even bother to count the desserts. We congeal everything. Instead of serving Smithfield ham with hot mustard, we serve it with a shimmering hot mustard mousse. Rare roast beef gets horseradish mousse sliced and stacked with the beef on homemade yeast rolls. For hors d'oeuvres, we would rather offer a molded Roquefort ring (Roquefort, chopped pecans, cream, and cream cheese) than mere Roquefort. Then there are the endless variations on tomato aspic, including my favorite—tomato soup aspic, a Junior League cookbook perennial made with canned tomato soup, mayonnaise, cream cheese, and sliced green olives.

I had always assumed that the Southerner's proclivity toward anything made with gelatin derived from the heat. All those smooth and glistening aspics and mousses would have provided cool relief. In fact, it wasn't until the advent of refrigeration that we could enjoy them during most of the year. "Jellies should never be made in hot weather," Marion Cabell Tyree warns in *Housekeeping in Old Virginia*, published in 1879. In *Dishes and Beverages of the Old South*, published in 1913, Martha McCulloch-Williams describes a typical wedding menu, adding that in cold weather, wine jelly "took the place of syllabub."

It turns out that our fondness for jelled foods comes from the British, who began making molded "jellies" as early as medieval times, when artistic cooks decorated them with edible gold and silver. Techniques for making them weren't perfected until toward the end of the eighteenth century when they became symbols of sophistication and status. No wonder. To make them was such a long and tedious process, only the wealthy could afford it. First, calves' feet and knuckles or hartshorn (deer antlers) were simmered in water for hours and allowed to cool, leaving a translucent jelly on the top. The jelly was further reduced by boiling, clarified with egg whites, and flavored with everything from fruit and wine or cream to ground meat or nuts. A typical example is "The Duchess of Montague's Receipt for Hartshorn Jelly" from an eighteenth-century manuscript found at Canons Ashby in Northamptonshire. In it, the cook is advised to "put in one gallon of water half a pound of Hartshorn. Let them boyl slowly till the Liquor is a pretty

strong Jelly, then strain it off and put in . . . the peel of eight oranges and four lemons, cut very thin, boyl it a quarter of an hour,
then put in the whites of 12 eggs . . . the Juice of the Oranges and
Lemons, and a pound and a quarter of double refined Sugar, boyl it
a little and then strain it through a Flannell Bagg."

In Colonial America, gelatin was not such an indicator of class.
In her cookbook, Tyree points out that it was easy for "country
housekeepers in particular to make this sort of jelly, as the materi-
als generally are within their reach." Isinglass, a jelling agent made
from the air bladders of sturgeon was also popular, and by the
1860s, some crude commercial gelatins (sold in paper-thin "leaves")
were available. Tyree was partial to Cox's Sparkling Gelatin, and
included it in recipes for blanc mange, Bavarian cream, charlotte
russe, "meat jelly for boned turkey," and "lemon froth." However,
Isinglass required almost as much boiling and straining as calves'
feet and hartshorn, and the early leaf gelatin was not always foolproof. Finally, in 1890 the process for making granulated commercial gelatin was perfected by Charles Knox, a fact that made him so
rich he bought the famous racehorse Anaconda and gave him the
unfortunate new moniker "Gelatine King."

While gelatin is defined in *The New Food Lover's Companion* as
"pure protein derived from beef and veal bones, cartilage, tendons,
and other tissue," most commercial gelatin today is a by-product of
pigskin. This information must be startling to those vegetarians
who ingest commercial ice cream, yogurt, gummy bears, and the
hundreds of other prepared foods containing gelatin, not to mention the "gel caps" that encase an increasing number of over-the-
counter medicines. Since I am not a vegetarian I am grateful for
those handy quarter-ounce envelopes of instant gelatin. My friends
and I spent much of our teen years drinking dissolved Knox

straight out of a glass in an effort to make our hair shiny and our nails strong. (These days there is a product called Knox for Nails.) But my devotion to Knox reached its apex just a few years ago, after I'd apparently lost my mind and tried jelling something the old-fashioned way.

I was in Bath, England, for the summer and in charge of organizing an enormous picnic to take to a country–house cricket match. One of the guests was originally from New Orleans and her favorite thing in life is daube glacé, a highly seasoned beef stew that is jellied and molded in a loaf pan. Served on crusty French bread with lots of homemade mayonnaise, it makes an extremely upscale and delicious New Orleans roast beef po'boy sandwich, and I was determined to show the Brits a thing or two. Maybe it was the English damp, or maybe it was all the hours of mind-numbing cricket I'd been forced to watch. At any rate I forgot all about Mr. Knox and followed the only recipe I could find in the Bath bookstore, which included plenty of calves' feet and veal knuckles but no granulated gelatin. It didn't work. After about eight hours of simmering and two days of refrigeration it ended up a sort of glutinous beef soup, which I finally heated up and served over noodles the day after the picnic.

I have since learned to forgo the animal parts and add four envelopes of gelatin (one envelope usually will jell about two cups of liquid). Now that I have perfected my daube glacé I intend to serve it at my own next house party, where I'll have no qualms about thickening the blood of my guests. Over the course of the weekend I'll probably also offer a tomato aspic ring filled with lump crabmeat or a curried rice salad, a boozy charlotte russe with homemade ladyfingers, Julia Child's divine chicken mousse with foie gras and truffles, and maybe even some wine jelly, although that is most often served during the Christmas holidays, in keeping with its original seasonal roots.

While I cook, I'll entertain myself by listening to Rogers and Hart—specifically "I Wish I Were in Love Again," surely the only song ever written that successfully incorporates the verb "congeal" into its lyrics. "When love congeals," Lorenz Hart wrote in one of his archer moments, "it soon reveals the faint aroma of performing seals." I will also raise a glass to the rather gauche Mr. Knox, whose gelatin has no aroma whatsoever, and when it congeals the result is not dull or disastrous, as in the song, but shimmering and divine.

CHARLOTTE RUSSE

YIELD: 8 TO 10 SERVINGS

. . .

½ cup milk

2 tablespoons unflavored gelatin

4 cups heavy cream

1½ cups sugar

5 eggs, separated

½ cup bourbon or brandy

Place the milk in a small saucepan and sprinkle with the gelatin. Set aside for 5 minutes to soften, then heat over low heat until dissolved. Set aside to cool.

In a large bowl, beat the cream with 1 cup of the sugar until firm peaks form when the beaters are raised. Set aside.

Place the egg yolks in a large bowl and gradually beat in remaining sugar. Beat at high speed for several minutes, until the mixture is thick and pale yellow. Stir in the gelatin and bourbon. With a rubber spatula, fold in one-fourth of the whipped cream to lighten the mixture; then fold in the remaining whipped cream.

In another large bowl, using clean beaters, beat the egg whites until soft peaks form when the beaters are raised; fold into the cream mixture. Line an 8-cup charlotte mold or a deep glass bowl with ladyfingers (preferably homemade), spoon in the cream mixture, and chill until set.

LADYFINGERS

. . .

1 tablespoon softened butter

2 tablespoons all-purpose flour

3 eggs, separated

½ cup plus 1 tablespoon granulated sugar

1 teaspoon vanilla extract

Pinch of salt

⅔ cup sifted all-purpose flour

¾ cup confectioners' sugar, in a shaker or sieve

Preheat the oven to 300 degrees. Line two baking sheets with parchment paper, or butter two baking sheets, dust with the 2 tablespoons flour, and shake off the excess.

Place the egg yolks in a 3-quart mixing bowl and gradually beat in the granulated sugar at high speed, until the mixture is thick and pale yellow. Beat in the vanilla.

In a medium bowl, using clean beaters, beat the egg whites and salt until soft peaks form when the beaters are raised. Scoop a fourth of the egg whites onto the egg-yolk mixture. Using a sifter or sieve, sift a fourth of the flour on top, and with a rubber spatula, fold the ingredients until partly blended. Repeat until all the egg whites are incorporated, but don't try to blend the mixture too thoroughly (the batter should remain light and puffy).

Using a spoon or pastry bag, spread or pipe the batter in 4 by 1½-inch strips spaced 1 inch apart onto the prepared baking sheets. Sprinkle with confectioners' sugar.

Bake the ladyfingers in the middle and upper third of the oven for about 20 minutes, or until very pale brown and slightly crusty on the outside. Remove immediately from the baking sheets and cool on a rack.

DAUBE GLACÉ

Adapted from The Plantation Cookbook,
by the Junior League of New Orleans

* * *

4 pounds boneless beef
    chuck roast
Salt
Freshly ground black
    pepper
3 tablespoons bacon grease
    or olive oil
4 cups dark veal stock
½ cup dry red wine
½ cup brandy
3 onions, peeled and sliced
3 carrots, peeled and sliced
1 cup chopped celery
8 garlic cloves, peeled
8 sprigs flat-leaf parsley

5 bay leaves
12 whole cloves, crushed
2 teaspoons whole white
    peppercorns
1 teaspoon dried thyme
1 teaspoon whole allspice
½ teaspoon cayenne pepper
1 cup water
4 envelopes (4 tablespoons)
    unflavored gelatin
2 tablespoons salt
5 tablespoons lemon juice
3 tablespoons
    Worcestershire sauce
½ teaspoon Tabasco sauce

Dry the meat with paper towels and sprinkle it with salt and pepper. In a large, heavy-bottom casserole, heat the bacon grease till smoking; sear the meat on all sides. Remove the meat; pour out the grease.

Return the meat to the casserole; add the veal stock, wine, brandy, vegetables, and spices. Cover, and heat the liquid to simmering over medium-low heat. Reduce the heat to very low, cover, and simmer for 3 hours, turning the meat if it's not completely submerged.

Remove the meat to a bowl; let stand till cool.

Trim the fat from the meat, and cut the meat into a ½-inch dice. Oil two 1½-quart loaf pans and spread half of the meat in each pan.

Pour the stock through a cheesecloth-lined strainer over a large bowl and skim off the fat. Set the stock aside.

Place 1 cup water in a small saucepan and sprinkle with the gelatin. Set aside for 5 minutes to soften, then heat over low heat until dissolved. Stir into the reserved stock. Add 2 tablespoons salt, the lemon juice, Worcestershire, and Tabasco; stir well and pour over the meat. Refrigerate till the stock is set.

To serve, remove any fat from the top of the jellied stock and unmold each loaf onto a serving platter. Slice with a sharp knife that has been dipped in hot water. For hors d'oeuvres, cut into small squares and serve on thin baguette slices with Creole mustard or homemade mayonnaise.

Stilettos in the Grass

❁

When I was very young, the woman who took care of me when my parents were away sat on the edge of my bed and sang, always, "He's Got the Whole World in His Hands" to put me to sleep. When it was her turn, my mother inexplicably chose the Johnny Mercer and Hoagy Carmichael tune, "In the Cool, Cool, Cool of the Evening." Coatee's rhythmic reassurances of the Lord's (and her own rather more palpable) protection always sent me straight to dreamland. But after my mother finished her song, I'd lie awake for hours imagining—yearning for, really—the party that was "getting a glow on," and the "singin'" that "fills the air." By the time I'd got around to "better save a chair," I had the whole scene in my head: a gilded ballroom chair waiting for me next to a dance floor on a wide green lawn. The orchestra would be playing, of course, and I'd arrive, late, "in the shank of the night/ when the doin's are right," trailing a white mink stole behind me. All the women would have on diamonds and gardenias and all the men would've already shed their white dinner jackets. I'd drink champagne out of those old-fashioned saucers and smoke cigarettes out of a holder, and faint tinklings of laughter would float in from discreet pockets farther afield, where all the trees would be hung with strings of white lights.

Invariably, the next morning I would wake up crushed that I had not somehow become at least twenty overnight, that it would be years before I would attend such a spectacular garden party. As it happened I didn't have to wait quite so long.

My first outdoor bash was a wedding where I was the rice girl. I wore batiste rather than fur, and I walked around passing bags of rice out of a painted wicker basket. But I was serious about my work, which had the added bonus of allowing my five-year-old self a close-up view of the adults' doings: who was smooching whom among the rose bushes, which woman *arrived* toting her stilletto-heeled sandals over her shoulder. When I was thirteen, that same bride's brother married, and I wore what remains one of the best-looking dresses I've ever owned: a thin cotton Cacharel print with fluttery cap sleeves and a tight bodice with a back cut to the waist. I bought it with two months' worth of earnings from sweeping the floors and affixing price tags onto the clothes at the same store where it was sold. Beneath its knife-pleated mid-calf skirt, I had on my first pair of evening sandals, strappy, cream, snakeskin Charles Jourdans that came on the bus all the way from Neiman Marcus's flagship store in Dallas. Grown women told me later that they were hideously jealous of me in that getup—if they'd only known that the next morning my mother put me on a bus to a Baptist Bible camp. She said I was becoming too cynical and sophisticated for my own good (a tad unfair when you consider that it was she who started it all by singing me that song), and the world of Johnny Mercer and clinking glasses vanished in an Alabama pine grove where even decks of cards were forbidden.

That lost world was reclaimed at a spectacular graduation party in Washington, D.C., thrown by the very regal and generous grandmother of one of my boarding school classmates. (The niece of the shah of Iran had initially offered to host it at the embassy, and we all had visions of caviar dancing in our heads until Khomeini had the bad manners to throw her uncle out just weeks before we graduated.) I danced on an enormous stone terrace that overlooked all of Washington in a floaty black-and-white, fern-print, chiffon dress and snaked another classmate's very good-looking boyfriend on the theory that, if it happens outside at night, it doesn't count, or at least it may be forgiven. The nice thing about lawns is that even in the daytime, they afford plenty of shadows to duck into.

The British may have invented garden parties, but theirs have never struck me as much fun—in the social pages of *Harpers & Queen*, the men usually have on morning coats and the women have on suits and too-big hats or stiff organza dresses. At the garden parties of my youth, the men wore suits of seersucker or poplin, and in New Orleans they still wear white linen with white bucks. My next-door neighbors used to have lots of afternoon parties in their backyard, which I would view from my perch in our pear tree. (Coatee would take a slat out of the fence and watch from a chair brought outside from the kitchen.) Once we watched in amazement as my father made figure eights on a friend's motorcycle and eventually hit a tree. My mother wore a gauzy, cream Dior tunic over a pair of matching pants that day, and I'm pretty sure my father would have had on the saddle oxfords that were part of his usual festive outdoor kit.

While it is great fun to choose the appropriate attire, the proper madcap spirit should also be donned. The other day I ran across *The Bon Vivant's Cookbook*, published by a man named William Templeton Veach in 1965, before the term *bon vivant*—and the thing itself—became archaic. It contains recipes perfect for garden parties, including ingenious cherry tomatoes halved, hollowed out, filled with tomato aspic, and topped with a dab of mayonnaise. "In summer serve in a dish set in cracked ice," the book advises. How fabulous alongside platters of cold lobster and oysters on the half shell and maybe a big old bowl of pristine osetra caviar and giant silver coolers containing Krug champagne.

Almost forty years have passed since I first imagined such a party. My fervent hope is that someone I know will have it finally and invite me. The bartender will know how to make a perfect Ramos gin fizz, and a big band will be playing, preferably Peter Duchin's. The vocalist will, naturally, be singing, "In the cool, cool, cool of the evening/Tell 'em I'll be there." And at last I will be.

CHERRY TOMATO CANAPÉS

» » »

70 to 80 cherry tomatoes

1 recipe frozen tomato aspic (recipe follows)

1 recipe homemade mayonnaise (see page 26)

With a sharp knife, shave a very thin slice off the bottom of each tomato so that it will sit level on a tray. Slice a fourth of each tomato off the top (just enough so that you have room to scoop out the insides), and discard the tops. Carefully scoop the flesh out of each tomato using a small melon baller and discard the flesh as well. The shells may be prepared in advance and stored in the refrigerator for a few hours.

When ready to serve, use the melon baller to scoop out balls of the frozen tomato aspic and carefully stuff it into the prepared tomato shells.

Top off the aspic with a dab of mayonnaise piped through a pastry tube. (The pastry tube will be neater, but you may also use your smallest measuring spoon to make a tiny dollop.)

FOR THE FROZEN TOMATO ASPIC

3 cups tomato juice

3 cups Hellmann's mayonnaise

1 small onion, finely chopped

¾ cup crushed pineapple

¼ cup cream cheese

¼ cup cottage cheese

1 tablespoon Worcestershire sauce

2 drops Tabasco, or more to taste

Red food coloring, if desired

Salt and white pepper

Combine 2 cups of the tomato juice, 1 cup of the mayonnaise, the onion, pineapple, cream cheese, cottage cheese, Worcestershire sauce, and Tabasco in a blender. Blend until smooth and pour into a bowl. Combine the remaining tomato juice and mayonnaise in a blender and blend until smooth. Add enough food coloring so that it is the color of a ripe tomato—otherwise it will be pale pink. Add it to the mixture in the bowl and whisk until combined. Season with salt and pepper. Pour into a 2-inch-deep baking dish (strain through a sieve if you want a smoother texture) and freeze.

NOTE: Veach's recipe called for using regular tomato aspic, which is a far trickier enterprise as you must take great care to make sure the tomato shells are leak-proof. With these canapés, I happen to like the taste and texture of the frozen tomato aspic, made famous at Nashville's Belle Meade Country Club, best. However, if you'd like to try it the other way—and it is a very chic presentation—make your favorite plain tomato aspic recipe (without any additions such as olives, celery, etc). Arrange the prepared tomato shells on a cookie sheet and carefully fill each shell almost to the top with the aspic. Refrigerate until set and garnish with mayonnaise as directed above.

RAMOS GIN FIZZ

* * *

2 ounces gin

1 ounce simple syrup

½ ounce fresh lemon juice

½ ounce fresh lime juice

1 egg white

1 ounce heavy cream

4 drops orange flower water

Chilled club soda

Combine the first seven ingredients in a cocktail shaker with ice.
Shake vigorously.
Strain into a highball glass and top off with club soda.

SIMPLE SYRUP

YIELD: 12 OUNCES

. . .

Combine one cup of water and one cup of sugar in a small saucepan and bring to a boil over medium-high heat, stirring to dissolve the sugar, about three minutes.

Remove from heat and let cool.

Syrup may be stored in a glass jar and refrigerated for up to one month.

The Literary Club

❖

There have been two occasions in my life when I have been motivated into the kitchen by literature. The first time it happened I was reading *Anna Karenina* in tandem with someone I loved very much, so when we got to part four, I decided to replicate Oblonsky's massive hors d'oeuvres buffet that facilitated the successful reunion of Levin and Kitty. There were six kinds of vodka and at least as many cheeses with silver spreaders, pickled mushrooms and shallots, beluga caviar with tiny mother-of-pearl spoons, various tinned delicacies, and sliced dark breads. The vodka got the best of us, of course, as did the tragic nature of Anna's—and our own—romance. Plied with booze and lust and fish eggs, we got into a heap of trouble that afternoon, with far-reaching ramifications, the least of which was my missing three different planes to somewhere I really needed to be.

The next instance was much less grand, and certainly less Russian in both scale and drama quotient, but also far more satisfying, since I remember the whole thing clearly. I was lying in bed, alone, early one Sunday morning reading *Edisto Revisited*, by Padgett Powell. I had just begun the book, and I was in a good mood because *Edisto* is one of my favorite novels. I was looking forward to a few pleasant hours in my nightgown, and then, on page 52, the hero makes a club sandwich for his new girlfriend. A few pages earlier he had put bacon on the griddle, and I handled that alright, but then he wrote: "She leaned over the expert lay of smart club sandwiches and kissed me: mayonnaise, bacon and salty girl. Or: tongue tomato tart and salty lip of girl. Or: tart tomato, salty lip and woman."

I was not interested in the lip or the girl/woman. It was all that talk of bacon, tomato, and mayonnaise, of that salty tart thing, and I knew I would not be happy until all that stuff was sliding around in my own mouth. So I got out of bed, dressed, drove to the store, and bought: thickly sliced bacon, the best tomato I could find, Pepperidge Farm white bread, a jar of Hellmann's mayonnaise, and a head of iceberg lettuce. A real club sandwich has chicken on it, but I was in too much of a hurry for that. I made a classic BLT instead, and it was possibly the best thing I have ever put in my mouth.

Powell's book is full of other food references. He makes soft scrambled eggs with heavy pepper and serves them with neat whiskey. He goes on at length about the excellent pairing of Smithfield ham with a gin and tonic. (It's that salty tart thing again.) But Powell is not the norm.

Most American literature is seriously devoid of culinary references, which is why it is such a pleasure to read Tolstoy. Proust may have written a million words based on memories prompted by a simple tea cake, but the madeleine really was not the point. In *Anna Karenina* on the other hand, Oblonsky (Anna's jolly brother) is so obsessed with food that it becomes almost another character. He is forever planning menus, confabbing with waiters, "peeling the sloshy oysters from their pearly shells with a little silver fork and swallowing them one after another." He revels in the joys of "superb but simple roast beef"; he forces sauces and Chablis on poor simple Levin.

In American fiction, those coming close to Oblonsky's obsession most often seem to be detectives. There is the vast and fussy gourmand, Nero Wolfe, and then there is Lawrence Sanders's appealing Delaney of the Deadly Sin series. The man cannot eat enough sandwiches. Even the people he's chasing eat them. *The First Deadly Sin* opens with a health-conscious serial murderer munching on stone-ground whole wheat with radishes and plum tomatoes.

Delaney's combinations are not always as tantalizing as those of Powell's protagonist. He eats chicken with red onion and black olive slices on rye with horseradish sauce. He eats "interracial sandwiches" including ham on a bagel, and "wet sandwiches" like the delicious-sounding potato salad and pastrami on rye with hot English mustard. He declares early on that he "dearly" loves mayonnaise. He even eats it "thinly spread on rye" with spiced salami, which I can't imagine, but I share his love of the stuff, especially when it is homemade.

My own madeleine is a tomato sandwich on white bread with homemade mayonnaise made by my grandmother's cook Eleanor, who died when I was seven. She always cut the bread in rounds to fit a single tomato slice, and sometimes she added finely chopped scallions to the mayonnaise, sometimes not. She made them for my cousin and me when my grandmother took us on outings, like to the trout farm where the ponds were ludicrously packed with fish. My grandmother would stand, in her Delman heels and cotton shirtdress, a bit away, with her alligator handbag firmly on her arm, looking exactly like Queen Elizabeth. We would fish and eat the sandwiches (actually I would eat the sandwiches; my cousin hates tomatoes) while my grandmother watched us through her dark glasses and smoked Pall Malls.

Whenever I eat a tomato sandwich, which is as often as possible, I think of Eleanor's tall, thin body and her wide, kind face, and of my grandmother smoking, but also of my first beloved literary heroine, Harriet the Spy. There is a scene in the book, which I reread all the time, in which the exasperated cook and Harriet's mother, Mrs. Welsch, are trying to get Harriet to change her school lunch choice of five straight years. "Wouldn't you like to try a ham sandwich, or egg salad, or peanut butter?" an increasingly hysterical Mrs. Welsch wants to know. "Tomato," Harriet says, not even looking up from the book she is reading at breakfast. They keep at it, suggesting cream cheese and olive, pastrami, roast beef, and cucumber, but Harriet calmly refuses to budge.

I identified with her from that moment on, just as I identified with Delaney and his love of mayonnaise on anything, just as I identified with Powell and his salty tart preoccupation. In all these cases, the mayonnaise is the key. (It is after all the perfect marriage of salty tart, since its two essential flavorings are lemon juice or vinegar and salt.) My mother makes the best homemade mayonnaise I have ever tasted. There is nothing that is not enhanced by it: club sandwiches, tomato sandwiches, cucumber sandwiches (especially cucumber sandwiches; plain cucumber sandwiches with butter are just about the most vapid things on the planet), thin-sliced turkey with black pepper, perhaps even Delaney's spiced salami. My mother also makes an incredibly hot and delicious mustard that would be really good on Delaney's pastrami with potato salad and absolutely perfect on a sandwich of Powell's Smithfield ham. This mustard and this mayonnaise make sandwiches good enough to write books about. Oblonsky would've loved them.

CLUB SANDWICHES

YIELD: 2 SANDWICHES

. . .

4 slices good white bread, either Pepperidge Farm or from
    a light homemade loaf
Homemade mayonnaise (see page 26)
2 to 4 thin slices breast of chicken, either roasted or
    poached, on the bone, for the occasion
Salt
Freshly ground black pepper
8 slices thick bacon, cooked until crisp
2 big slices lettuce, either iceberg, romaine, or Boston (I
    love Boston best on this)
1 tomato

Lightly toast the bread and spread it generously with mayonnaise (preferably homemade). Add 1 or 2 thin slices of chicken, and sprinkle with salt and freshly ground black pepper. Add 4 pieces of bacon, lettuce to cover the bacon, followed by thin slices of tomato. Lightly salt and pepper the tomato. Top with the second piece of toast, mayonnaise side down. Repeat. Cut both sandwiches in half and serve.

NOTE: A true club sandwich is supposed to have another slice of bread in the middle of the filling, but I think it gets in the way of the flavor. Also, people love to add other fillings to this classic combination—avocado, sprouts, cheese. But, again, they screw up the balance. When making sandwiches, too much is not a good thing. However, avocado can be substituted for the chicken to good effect, especially if you add a bit of canned chipotle pepper paste to the mayonnaise along with a bit of chopped cilantro. It's almost as good as the original.

MAYONNAISE

YIELD: 1 1/4 CUPS

. . .

1 teaspoon salt

1 teaspoon Coleman's dry mustard

1/2 teaspoon sugar

2 egg yolks

2 tablespoons lemon juice

1 cup Wesson oil

Pinch of cayenne pepper

Mix the first three ingredients together in the bottom of a mixing bowl. Add the egg yolks and 1 tablespoon of the lemon juice and beat until pale yellow. Add the oil in droplets. When the mayonnaise begins to emulsify, add the oil in a thin, steady stream, pausing as it thickens to add the second tablespoon of lemon juice. Taste to make sure it has enough lemon and salt, and add the cayenne.

NOTE: My mother makes this in her ancient KitchenAid on the slowest speed, which achieves almost the same results as a whisk. Almost anything other than a slow mixer or a whisk goes too fast, resulting in mayonnaise that is too tight. I have done it with a hand mixer, but you still need to slow it down a bit by whisking in between. I know people swear by blenders and food processors, but the texture is never as good, and often to make it work, you have to throw in a whole egg, which alters the taste.

CUCUMBER SANDWICHES

* * *

1 cucumber, sliced into rounds
1 small white onion, peeled and sliced
½ cup cider vinegar
2 heaping tablespoons sugar
Thinly sliced white or wheat bread
Homemade mayonnaise (page 26)

1. Place the cucumber, onion, vinegar, and sugar in a bowl and toss to mix. Add enough water to cover, along with a few cubes of ice. Soak the cucumbers for at least an hour or overnight (they will keep refrigerated for several days).

2. Drain. With a 2-inch biscuit or cookie cutter, cut the bread into rounds the size of the cucumber slices. (One piece of bread is enough for two rounds.) Spread one side of each round with mayonnaise and place a cucumber slice between the two rounds, mayonnaise sides in.

HOT MUSTARD

YIELD: 2 1/4 CUPS

1 cup Coleman's dry mustard

1 cup cider vinegar

1 cup sugar

3 eggs, beaten well

Mix the mustard with the vinegar in a stainless steel bowl, cover, and allow to soak overnight.

Add enough water to the bottom of a double boiler to hold the top container without it touching the water. Bring the water to a boil. Lower to a steady simmer and add the mustard-vinegar mixture to the top part of the double boiler. Add the sugar and eggs, stirring constantly until the mixture thickens. Remove the mustard from the heat, let cool, and refrigerate. The mustard will be like a thick soup, but will thicken considerably when refrigerated.

Green Party

When I got married, my friend Elaine Shannon sent me a stack of wonderful old Southern cookbooks, which prompted a lively e-mail correspondence about the food we both grew up eating. In one of her dispatches, Elaine, who is from Georgia, reported that her grandmother had two biases about food: roast beef had to be cooked until it fell apart, and she couldn't abide collard greens. To her, Elaine wrote, "collards were worse than useless, and any house where they had been cooked had to be burned to the ground. She was a turnip-greens woman."

I didn't know it at the time, but my own mother, until recently, was one, too. (She grew up in Nashville, a place described in *Nashville: Personality of a City* as "the turnip-greens and hog-jowl center of the universe." Alfred Leland Crabb writes, "These two were used in fitting combination . . . by 1810, and the townspeople's appetite for them has not waned.") I discovered her allegiance before a recent Thanksgiving. I was the cook that year and I called her from the produce aisle to ask how many people were coming so I'd be sure to get enough collards. "*Collards?*" she roared with such disgust I almost dropped my cell phone. "They are tough and, well, just awful." I responded that I had recently eaten some of my friend

Robert Carter's braised collards at the superlative Peninsula Grill in Charlston, South Carolina, and that they were some of the most delicious things I had ever tasted. She was unimpressed and told me that I had best bring home some turnip and mustard greens, too.

I had no idea there were such passionate greens factions. I guess since the South lost the war, its residents have to find things to argue about among themselves. I managed to negotiate a peace in my own family by quietly going on and making Carter's collards anyway, and now everybody's a convert. I'm not so sure I could have convinced Elaine's grandmother, but at least she wouldn't have had to burn down the house.

In her day, the only way people cooked greens was to boil them with a ham hock or a piece of slab bacon for hours until the house smelled so sour that it was indeed almost uninhabitable. Since collards are thicker than mustards or turnips, they cooked the longest and the stench was the worst. But in Carter's recipe, they aren't boiled to death, but braised for just fifteen minutes or so in degreased ham stock. Not only is there no stench, but you also get the great pork flavor that is such a complement to the greens without the fat.

In *The Gift of Southern Cooking,* Scott Peacock writes that he grew up in Alabama, where they were "segregationists," favoring turnip greens over all others, while his co-author, Edna Lewis, who hails from Virginia, took the more democratic approach of mixing lots of greens up in one pot. Their recipe follows her tradition, cooking such "Southern" greens as mustard and turnip with more widely grown varieties like watercress, escarole, kale, and chard. They boil theirs, but, like Carter, they do it in degreased pork stock and only for fifteen to twenty minutes.

Inspired by her Jeffersonian attitude, I made that recipe the day after Thanksgiving, and I don't think I've ever seen my father so happy. Any time he gets to eat greens—of any kind—two days in a row, he considers himself extremely lucky, and he is not alone. In 1984 at the annual Collard Festival in Ayden, North Carolina, a man named C. Mort Horst set a world record by eating seven and a half pounds of collard greens in thirty minutes. (However, it was reported that he kept them down just long enough to claim his prize.) A year later, a woman named Colleen Bunting contributed to an anthology devoted to collards called *Leaves of Green: The Collard Poems*. In one of the poems, she addresses Elaine's grandmother's prejudice: "Some say collards don't smell so nice,/But eat them once and you'll eat them twice."

An earlier poet named Cotton Noe wrote in 1912 that "I have never tasted meat,/Nor cabbage, corn nor beans,/ Nor fluid food one half as sweet/As that first mess of greens." The great Tony Joe White had a hit song in the late 1960s called "Polk Salad Annie." Poke sallet is a wild green and hard to come by these days, but the song remains a personal favorite because of its chorus, which includes the immortal phrase " 'cause her mama was working on a chain gang."

All of the above writers would have been referring to greens cooked the old-fashioned way and served with the classic accompaniment of cornbread, which is useful for dipping into the much-prized pot liquor. Pot liquor has plenty of nutrients; some people have been known to eat bowls of it by itself as a sort of soup. It also was useful to Senator Huey P. Long as filibuster material. In David Leon Chandler's *The Natural Superiority of Southern Politicians*, the author quotes from some of Long's more memorable rants devoted to blocking various pieces of legislation from the Roosevelt White House. At one point, the senator, who hailed, of course, from

Louisiana, dictated the recipe for pot liquor into the Congressional Record: "First let me tell the senators what pot liquor is. Pot liquor is the residue that remains from the commingling, heating, and evaporation . . . anyway it is in the bottom of the pot." He went on to hold up a wastebasket to demonstrate how to properly put turnip greens into a pot, and followed up with instructions on how to make both a Sazerac cocktail and oysters Rockefeller.

Pot liquor is full of nutrients because the greens themselves are. Collards and their close relatives mustard greens and kale are an excellent source of calcium, iron, and vitamins A and C. (Mustards also contain thiamine and riboflavin, and the peak season for all three is December through March or April.) Chard, a member of the beet family, has much the same nutrients as its cruciferous cousins, plus phosphorous. It also has a less pronounced flavor so it's good to mix it with other, more peppery greens like mustards or watercress, and the French like to use it in gratins with eggs and milk and sometimes Gruyère or Parmesan.

Greens also have almost no calories, so without the addition of the pork they are the perfect diet food. My best friend, Jessica Brent, has come up with a healthy way to prepare them that is so good it satisfies even such die-hard traditionalists like my father. She puts three or four bunches of cleaned and stemmed mustard greens in a big pot with a half cup of olive oil, two cups of dry white wine, and salt to taste and steams them until they are tender, about twenty minutes. The vegetarian chef Deborah Madison braises collards or turnip greens in brown butter and does a wonderful recipe of twelve cups of mixed greens sautéed in olive oil with garlic, a cup of chopped parsley, a cup of chopped cilantro, and two teaspoons each of paprika and ground cumin.

Some people, though, really miss their pork. In Afghanistan, I met an American aid worker who grew kale in her garden there, and all she could talk about was how much better it would be if she could only get her hands on some bacon. For folks like her, I offer two recipes: Robert Carter's collards with country ham, and one for mustards braised with bacon from Donald Link at New Orleans's very fine Herbsaint. Kale could be used successfully in both.

ROBERT CARTER'S BRAISED COLLARD GREENS

YIELD: 6 SERVINGS

(PORK STOCK YIELD: ABOUT 9 CUPS)

⁘

FOR THE COLLARD GREENS

1 pound collard greens, cleaned and stemmed

2 tablespoons olive oil

¼ cup (about ¾ ounce) country ham, cut in thin strips

2 tablespoons minced shallots

⅓ cup aged sherry vinegar

⅓ cup tupelo honey

½ cup Smoked Pork Stock (recipe follows)

Salt

Freshly ground pepper to taste

¼ cup butter

FOR THE SMOKED PORK STOCK

2 pounds ham hocks or a 2-pound piece of Smithfield ham
    or other cured country ham

To make the collard greens: Cut the collard greens into a chiffonade, about ½ inch wide, and blanch in salted boiling water for 10 seconds. Drain, refresh in ice water, and squeeze dry.

Heat the oil in a large sauté pan over medium heat. Add the ham and shallots and sauté. Deglaze the pan with the sherry vinegar and stir in the honey. Add the stock and bring to a simmer.

Add the collard greens and cook at a healthy simmer until tender, 10 to 15 minutes. Using a slotted spoon, remove the greens to a bowl. Bring the cooking liquid to a boil and cook until reduced to about ¼ cup. Add salt and pepper. Taste and adjust the seasonings. (You may want to add a little more honey or vinegar.) Add the butter, stirring constantly until it melts. Return the greens to the pan and toss to coat with the butter.

NOTE: Tupelo honey is available at Gourmet Garage and Dean & DeLuca.

To make smoked pork stock: Rinse the ham hocks or ham and set in a large stockpot. Add 1 gallon of water. Cook, covered, at a full simmer for at least 2 hours, or until the stock develops a strong flavor. Strain and discard the meat. (Or use the meat to make ham salad or to flavor soups or beans.)

Cook the stock completely, and skim off the fat. (Ham hocks will produce more fat.) The stock may be refrigerated for up to a week or frozen for six months.

BACON-BRAISED MUSTARD GREENS

Adapted from Donald Link, Herbsaint Restaurant

YIELD: 4 TO 6 SERVINGS

• • •

2 or 3 bunches mustard greens (about 3¾ pounds total; 16
   cups trimmed)
8 ounces thickly sliced lean slab bacon, diced
1 large onion, diced (about 2 cups)
1 teaspoon chopped garlic
1 teaspoon hot red pepper flakes
3 tablespoons sugar
½ cup apple cider vinegar
½ cup chicken stock
Salt
Freshly ground black pepper

Rinse the greens well. Cut out the stems and thick veins, and
tear the leaves into 4- or 5-inch pieces.

Cook the bacon in a large sauté pan until the fat starts to ren-
der and the bacon begins to brown. Add the onion, garlic, and red
pepper flakes and sauté until the onion is soft, about 7 minutes.
Add the sugar, vinegar, and chicken stock. Heat to boiling, add the
greens, and cook slowly, stirring often as the greens begin to release
their own liquid.

Reduce the heat and simmer the greens until tender, 10 to 20
minutes, stirring occasionally. Season with salt and pepper to taste.

Mellow Yellow

❖

When I was growing up, the most exotic thing anybody could possibly serve was a chicken or shrimp curry. This was in the 60s, long before we had ever heard of red or green Thai curries. And certainly long before home cooks thought to make their own freshly roasted and hand-ground blends of spices. A "curry" was a dish made with marigold yellow curry powder straight from the jar, blended with heavy cream or coconut milk, and served with at least a dozen little bowls of delicious condiments ranging from chutney to crumbled bacon and chopped bananas. Its foreign associations put it in the same exalted league of dinner-party fare as, say, chicken Kiev, but its flavors were more nuanced and its presentation was far more festive.

When I was fourteen and going off to France for a month, chicken curry was featured at the farewell dinner party that our friends the Hardings gave in my honor. A few years later, when I was in college and in need of a menu to serve to some full-fledged adults, my hostess sent me her recipe, carefully typed on pale blue monogrammed stationery. I still use the same one, covered now with oily yellow blotches, and I still remember the first time I made it, pushing the sauce through a strainer while sitting on the floor of my primitive kitchen. Since then, I have come to realize that the curry of my childhood is indeed an old Southern dish but from southern India, by way of England.

The word *curry*, loosely translated from the Indian *kari* to mean sauce, became the catchall term for any of the hot, spicy, gravy-based dishes Europeans first tasted in India. The first commercial curry powder represented an attempt to replicate the curry blends of southern India, which vary dramatically depending on the region and the cook, and which can include up to twenty spices, herbs, and seeds. Among the most commonly used are cardamom, chile, cinnamon, cloves, coriander, cumin, fennel seed, fenugreek, mace, mustard seeds, nutmeg, red and black pepper, poppy seeds, saffron, tamarind, and turmeric, which gives it the bright yellow color. The British in India became so fond of the stuff that there was a great demand for it in commercial form, and the same basic mixture has been available since the late eighteenth century.

By the close of the nineteenth century, curry powder was so popular in England that Law's Grocer's Manual listed a dozen recipes for it, and it had even followed English settlers to America. In *Mrs. Hill's New Cook Book*, published in 1872, there is a recipe for curry soup, one for curry sauce, two for "veal cutlets curried" and one for "veal with curry powder," also said to be "excellent" with chicken and turtle.

But the most famous of the Anglo-Indian-Southern dishes is Country Captain. Georgians have always claimed that a sea captain in the spice trade gave the recipe to friends in the port of Savannah, but it's more likely that the British colonials brought it over. Either way, local enthusiasm for the dish made it a mainstay in Georgia kitchens. And in the 1940s, a hostess named Mrs. W. L. Bullard from Warm Springs, Georgia, is said to have served it at a dinner for F.D.R., which added considerably to its cachet.

Now of course Southerners and practically everybody else add a dash of curry to almost everything. I don't think I ever went to a cocktail party in my hometown where curry dip wasn't on a table surrounded by crudités. I serve it now at my own parties with steamed asparagus (the colors look great together). At brunches, my mother invariably serves hot curried fruit, a casserole of pineapple, pears, peaches, and apricots coated with a mixture of melted butter, brown sugar, and curry powder—a dish that is as good with eggs and country ham and cheese grits as it is with a braised pork roast. A more elegant side to roasts is my new favorite discovery, a simple cauliflower puree with just a dash of curry. It turns such a pale yellow that at first nobody can figure out what it is. Then even people who profess to hate cauliflower can't get enough of it.

These days I am well acquainted with the vast array of curries at my local Thai restaurant, and I have even made my own curry blends from the wonderful recipes of Madhur Jaffrey. But I am still a huge fan of the humble store-bought curry powder, a generous gift from one former British colony to another.

FRANKIE HARDING'S CHICKEN OR SHRIMP CURRY

YIELD: 6 SERVINGS

. . .

FOR THE SAUCE

3 tablespoons unsalted
butter

1 medium onion, peeled
and finely chopped

1 medium carrot, peeled
and thinly sliced

1 celery rib, thinly sliced

3 to 4 tablespoons hot
curry powder (like
Madras)

½ teaspoon chili powder

3 tablespoons all-purpose
flour

1 can (about 14 ounces)
coconut milk

½ teaspoon salt

⅛ teaspoon ground mace

⅛ teaspoon ground
allspice

⅛ teaspoon ground
nutmeg

⅛ teaspoon ground cloves

⅛ teaspoon ground
cinnamon

1 Rome or McIntosh apple,
chopped

2 tablespoons currant jelly

2 tablespoons mango
chutney, pureed in food
processor or blender

FOR THE CURRY

1½ pounds skinless, boneless chicken breasts, freshly
poached in simmering stock until just cooked through
(about 4 minutes) and cubed, or 1½ pounds medium
shrimp, steamed until just pink (about 3 minutes),
peeled and deveined (reserve cooking broth or shrimp
steaming liquid)

Heavy cream, optional

Cooked white basmati rice (allow 1½ cups per person)

4 slices cooked bacon, crumbled

3 scallions, finely chopped

3 jalapeño peppers, seeded and minced

1 crisp apple (like Fuji), coarsely chopped

1 hard-boiled egg, white and yolk sieved separately

½ cup coarsely chopped cashews, peanuts, or pistachios, toasted

½ cup mango chutney

½ cup shredded coconut, toasted

½ green bell pepper, finely chopped

1 banana, coarsely mashed just before serving

To make the sauce: Melt the butter in a 3-quart saucepan over medium-low heat. Add the onion, carrot, and celery and cook, stirring occasionally, until soft, about 5 minutes. Add the curry and chili powders and cook, stirring, for 5 minutes. Whisk in the flour, coconut milk, and ⅓ cup water, raise the heat to medium, and whisk until just boiling. Whisk in the salt, mace, allspice, nutmeg, cloves, cinnamon, and then the chopped apple. Reduce the heat to low, cover, and simmer for 30 minutes. Push the mixture through a strainer with a metal spoon into a medium bowl. Cover and refrigerate overnight.

When ready to serve, place the sauce in a saucepan and stir in the currant jelly and mango chutney. Heat over medium heat until blended, whisking occasionally. Add the cooked chicken or shrimp, stir, and cook until heated through, about 5 minutes. If the mixture is too thick, thin with some of the reserved chicken or shrimp cooking liquid, or heavy cream. Serve with the rice and the condiments in separate bowls.

PUREE OF CAULIFLOWER
WITH CURRY

. . .

One 2-pound head cauliflower

2 tablespoons unsalted butter, softened, plus more if
    desired

3 teaspoons hot curry powder (like Madras)

½ teaspoon salt

⅛ teaspoon ground white pepper

Heavy cream, optional

Trim off the leaves and cut out the central core of the cauliflower. Break the cauliflower into florets. Peel the core and slice
crosswise. Halve the florets lengthwise.

Bring ½ cup water to a boil in a 2-quart saucepan over medium
heat. Add the sliced core and florets and cook, covered, until tender, about 5 minutes.

Drain the cauliflower pieces, reserving the cooking liquid, and
place in a food processor. Add ¼ cup of the reserved cooking liquid, the butter, curry powder, salt, and pepper and puree to the desired consistency, adding more cooking liquid or more butter, if
desired. (I like this puree a bit rough, but you can puree it until
smooth and add a bit of heavy cream for a richer and more elegant-
looking side dish.) Check the seasonings and adjust if necessary.
Serve immediately or turn the puree into a gratin dish and reheat
in a 250-degree oven when ready to serve.

COUNTRY CAPTAIN

YIELD: 4 SERVINGS

* * *

½ cup currants

1 cup warm chicken stock

4 strips bacon

One 5-pound fryer, cut into 8 serving pieces, or 4 whole chicken breasts (with skin and bones attached), (about 12 to 14 ounces each)

⅓ cup all-purpose flour, seasoned with ¼ teaspoon salt and ⅛ teaspoon black pepper

2 celery ribs, finely chopped

2 medium yellow onions, peeled and finely chopped

1 medium green bell pepper, seeded and finely chopped

2 garlic cloves, peeled, and minced

2 cups fresh or drained canned tomatoes, peeled, cored, and chopped

1 tablespoon hot curry powder (like Madras)

2 teaspoons dark brown sugar

½ teaspoon salt

½ teaspoon dried thyme

½ teaspoon ground mace

½ teaspoon ground black pepper

¼ teaspoon ground white pepper

½ cup slivered almonds, toasted

1 teaspoon finely chopped flat-leaf parsley

Steamed white long-grain rice

In a small bowl, cover the currants with warm chicken stock. Set aside.

Fry the bacon in a nonstick skillet over medium heat until

crisp. Drain on paper towels, crumble, and reserve. Drain all but 3 tablespoons of the bacon grease from the pan.

Heat the grease remaining in the skillet over medium heat. Dredge the chicken in seasoned flour and shake off the excess. Cook the chicken in the grease until tender, about 30 minutes, turning the pieces frequently for uniform browning.

Preheat the oven to 325 degrees. Remove the chicken to a bowl. Add the celery, onions, bell pepper, and garlic to the drippings in the pan. Sauté the vegetables for about 5 minutes. Strain the stock from the currants and add it to the skillet along with the tomatoes, curry, brown sugar, salt, thyme, mace, and pepper.

Stir the tomato mixture, bring to a boil, and reduce the heat to low. Cover and simmer for about 10 minutes.

Place the chicken pieces in a large shallow baking dish, cover with the tomato mixture, and bake for 30 minutes. Sprinkle with the reserved currants, almonds, chopped parsley, and crumbled bacon. Return it to the oven and bake for 10 to 15 minutes more. Serve hot with steamed rice.

CURRY DIP

* * *

2 cups Hellman's mayonnaise

2 tablespoons Durkee sauce

2 tablespoons Heinz ketchup

1 tablespoon Worcestershire sauce

3 teaspoons curry powder (like Madras)

1 teaspoon Tabasco sauce

2 tablespoons finely grated onion

1 garlic clove, pressed

1 tablespoon prepared horseradish

1 teaspoon celery seed

pinch salt

Combine all the ingredients and keep refrigerated.

Applause, Applause

❖

I have three cookbooks from the 50s and 60s whose titles all but declare that cooking and entertaining are mostly about seduction, or at least about showing off: *The Perfect Hostess Cookbook,* (by Mildred O. Knopf), *Come for Cocktails, Stay for Supper* (by Lois Levine and Marian Burros), and my favorite, *Cooking for Compliments.* The author of the last one, a radio personality named Martha Deane, gets right to the point. "We may as well admit that it's fun to be complimented," she writes in her preface. "Possibly a sterner generation took a dim view of this thought, fearing that it smacked of the sin of vanity. But modern psychiatrists tell us that happy is she who reaps satisfaction from the work she does. Including her cooking—of which she will average some 50,000 hours of her married life!"

I realize that Deane published her book in 1954, but by her math, women were in the kitchen almost three hours a day, every day, for fifty years. I have never wanted a compliment that badly. I have, however, done my comparatively limited share of cooking for them.

When I was in college in Washington, and working in *Newsweek*'s bureau there, almost all of my friends were older and far, far more accomplished. They had hundreds of by-lines to my half-dozen or so, had written books and covered wars and lived in foreign countries. The only place I could come close to matching—or maybe even besting—their achievements was in the kitchen, so I tried mightily, giving endless brunches, lunches, cocktail parties, and dinners. I slaved for hours over things like coulibiacs of salmon and roulades of veal, took up nouvelle cuisine, and spent more money than I made. (I did not yet have a credit card, but I had a charge account at Georgetown's Neam's Market, which, tragically, no longer exists.) Finally, over the phone one day, after a particularly drawn-out menu-planning session, my mother lost patience and said, "Why don't you just serve something that tastes really good?"(This reminds me of what a friend of my grandfather's from Nashville, Tennessee, said to his daughter after she and her mother had agonized, in front of him, for hours over what she should wear to a costume party: "Jesus Christ, Polly, why don't you just put a raisin in your navel and go as a cookie?" But I digress.)

Anyway, I tried to relax. I turned back to Julia Child, and the *Joy of Cooking*, and the recipes I'd copied over from my mother before I'd left home. I made chocolate mousse, and leg of lamb, and lemon ice cream in an old-fashioned mold. I went to a dinner party at the gorgeous house of legendary Georgetown hostess and writer Susan Mary Alsop and was amazed to find that she served nothing more complicated than delicious crisp slices of sugared bacon (bacon!) for hors d'oeuvres and perfect rare roast beef as a main course. I attended a dinner given by her ex-husband Joe, the equally legendary gourmand and columnist, and was even more amazed to find out that his excellent spinach soufflé had actually been made by Stouffer's and his desserts were as simple and as American as homemade apple pie. At both tables, people raved.

They, like my mother, knew what Martha Deane espoused to

her readers. "Flair and the complicated aren't synonymous. Nor does the budget have to mount alarmingly to bring new interest to the menu. . . . What we need is to find the good idea, the praise-provoking recipe, and make it ours. This too, is art in cookery."

Years later, when I launched a fresh round of cooking for compliments in earnest, I had dozens of "praise-provoking" recipes under my belt. This time though, it was during a courtship, a long one, almost ten years off and on, during which time I probably did rack up at least one thousand hours in front of the stove. But I did not make myself crazy with coulibiacs of salmon. Instead I fried hundreds of chickens and made quarts of potato salad; I grilled thick rib eyes marinated Roman style in olive oil and rosemary and garlic; I did what I hate to do and baked bread. I begged hunters for wild ducks for gumbo and made Roquefort *gougères* as canapés with drinks. I've often wondered if I would have continued this performance had we actually ended up together. And though I loved doing it, it was definitely a performance. The beneficiary rather meanly called it my "geisha act," but I remember him complaining bitterly one day after his own culinary efforts had gone unremarked upon. He and a friend had cooked for two other guests who got too drunk to notice the artful presentation of the shrimp rémoulade with hearts of palm or to notice the care that had gone into the quail with dirty rice. He had been cooking for compliments, too. We all do.

The most successful meal of that era was a meltingly delicious barbecued veal shoulder from Lee Bailey, green beans and new potatoes cooked with ham hocks and served warm in a lemony vinaigrette, cornbread, and the best squash casserole on the planet earth (from fabulous Houston hostess Nancy Peterkin, who has no less than four kitchens in her house). It worked so well on the man in question that he came for cocktails and stayed not just for dinner, but for the next four or five meals in a row. I made it again for a Sunday lunch during a literary festival in New Orleans, and the writer Edmund White pronounced it the best meal he'd eaten during his stay, a high compliment indeed, since he had already eaten in some of the city's finest restaurants.

It is hardly a fancy menu, but if I were Martha Deane, I would include it among my "Fame-makers," the title of her last chapter, which does not, inexplicably, include a recipe for stuffed eggs. Whenever I serve them people are literally speechless in the face of their lusciousness, especially people who are used to being passed trays of overly complicated but comparatively tasteless canapés. My friend the food stylist and culinary historian Rick Ellis is responsible for this particular fame-maker. Rick executed and styled the Edith Wharton–era feast in Martin Scorcese's *Age of Innocence*, replete with fancy molded jellies and roast game, but when he entertains at home (at least when he's making these unbelievably good eggs), he cooks with the rule of another friend of mine in mind, that compliments generally increase according the cream-butter-mayonnaise quotient.

He also cooks according to Deane's dictum that "excellence is often found in simple things." It just takes awhile to figure that out.

BARBECUED VEAL

Adapted from Lee Bailey's Country Weekends

YIELD: 6 TO 8 SERVINGS

∗ ∗ ∗

1 boneless veal shoulder
(about 5 pounds)
2 bunches scallions,
trimmed, some tops
included, cut in half
1 large yellow onion, cut
into chunks
1 green bell pepper, cut
into chunks
8 sprigs flat-leaf parsley,
roughly chopped
3 large garlic cloves,
peeled

½ cup peanut oil
½ cup canned tomato
sauce
½ cup red wine or sherry
vinegar
¼ cup Worcestershire sauce
¼ cup honey
1 tablespoon capers,
drained
1 teaspoon salt
½ teaspoon freshly ground
black pepper
¼ teaspoon Tabasco sauce

Unroll the veal shoulder. Place it in a deep baking dish. Set aside.

Place the scallions, yellow onion, bell pepper, parsley, and garlic in a food processor and pulse until the mixture is cut to medium-size bits.

Heat the oil over medium heat in a skillet and add the contents of the food processor. Simmer for 5 minutes and stir in the remaining ingredients. Simmer for 20 minutes more. Taste and adjust the seasonings, and cool.

Completely cover the veal with the vegetable mixture. Cover and refrigerate for at least 5 hours, or overnight, turning the meat once or twice.

About an hour before cooking, remove the meat from the refrigerator. Prepare coals for a barbecue or heat a gas grill. Preheat the oven to 375 degrees. When the grill is ready, remove the meat from the marinade and grill each side for 15 minutes, turning frequently to keep the meat from burning.

Meanwhile, heat the marinade. Place the meat in a deep casserole, pour the sauce around it, and cover. Bake in the preheated oven for 1 hour. If still tough, bake up to 30 minutes more. Spoon some sauce over each serving and serve the rest of the sauce on the side.

NANCY PETERKIN'S SUMMER-SQUASH CASSEROLE

YIELD: 8 TO 10 SERVINGS

* * *

7 tablespoons butter

2 pounds yellow summer
squash

1 large onion, chopped

1 large garlic clove, chopped

½ red bell pepper, chopped

½ green bell pepper, chopped

1 jalapeño pepper, seeded
and chopped, optional

4 slices plain white bread,
toasted

24 Ritz crackers, crumbed in
food processor

½ pound sharp cheddar
cheese, grated

4 large eggs, beaten

½ cup heavy cream

1 teaspoon sugar

1 teaspoon salt

¼ teaspoon cayenne pepper

Preheat the oven to 350 degrees. Butter a 2½-quart baking dish. Cut the squash into ½-inch-thick slices. Cook the slices in boiling, salted water until tender, about 10 minutes. Drain. Puree the squash in a food processor.

Melt 6 tablespoons of the butter over medium heat. Add the onion, garlic, and peppers and cook until just tender. Meanwhile, crumb the toast in a food processor, melt the remaining tablespoon of butter, and toss together with the bread crumbs.

Mix the squash puree, cracker crumbs, sugar, and seasonings. Blend well. Pour the puree into the baking dish, top with the bread crumbs, and bake until browned, about 40 minutes.

DEVILED EGGS

YIELD: 24 DEVILED EGGS

1 dozen medium eggs

¼ cup mayonnaise

¼ cup Dijon mustard

4 tablespoons butter, at room temperature

1 teaspoon fresh lemon juice

¼ teaspoon cayenne pepper

Salt

Freshly ground white pepper

Finely snipped fresh chives for garnish

Place the eggs in a pan large enough to hold them in a single layer and cover with cold water. Bring to a boil, cover, turn off the heat, and let the eggs sit for 15 minutes. Drain and run under cold water until the eggs are completely cold.

Peel the eggs and cut in half lengthwise. Remove the yolks and rub through a fine-mesh strainer into a bowl. Add the mayonnaise, mustard, and butter; mix until smooth. Stir in the lemon juice, cayenne, salt, and white pepper to taste. Put the yolk mixture in a pastry bag or Ziploc bag with a cut-off corner.

Neatly pipe the mixture into the egg white halves by pressing on the bag. Sprinkle the eggs with the chives.

My Blue Heaven

❁

For almost a quarter of my life, I was so madly in love with a
Cancer, it almost killed me. No wonder they are represented
in the zodiac by a crab. Just like their crustacean counterparts,
Cancers move mostly sideways, and they change directions with no
notice—or worse, they simply retreat into their shells. They can indeed be "crabby," which Webster's defines as cross or ill-tempered,
and "crabbed" (morose and peevish), and they are very adept at
"crabbing" (making sour) what were, just moments earlier, the best
of times. They are moody and sensitive and vulnerable, and you
want to kill them, but they are saved by the fact that they also share
the crab's more irresistible nature. Once you have had a taste of
what lies beneath that hard and occasionally difficult shell, you find
that it is more than worth the patience and the hassle. And that it
is damn near impossible not to keep coming back for more.

What lies beneath the blue crab, found along the Atlantic and
Gulf Coasts, is, to use one of my father's favorite expressions, "a little
piece of paradise"—or, actually, several pieces. In fish stores, the best
of what the blue crab has to offer, the solid chunks of sweet white
meat from the back fin, is marked "jumbo lump," but it should be la-
beled "food of the gods." Mary J. Rathbun of the Smithsonian Institution knew what she had on her hands when she gave the blue crab

its scientific name, *Callinectes sapidus* Rathbun. In Greek, *callinectes* means beautiful swimmer (which this crab is), and *sapidus* means savory in Latin. Rathbun identified and described 998 crab species in her time, but the only crab she named savory was the blue.

Given the blue crab's scientific status and the gorgeous appearance of its pristine white lumps, not much should be added to it when cooking except those ingredients that highlight its already rich goodness. One of the most irritating things on a plate is a crab cake full of bread crumbs or mayonnaise or some other filler that has turned the noble crab into a patty of mush. Holding a crab cake together is a problem, though. Georges Perrier, the brilliant French chef who presides over Le Bec-Fin and Brasserie Perrier in Philadelphia, has an elegant solution. He purees raw shrimp in the food processor until it is shiny (it looks exactly like boiled, seven-minute, cake icing) and stiff enough to act as a binder for the crab. He adds seasonings, makes the cakes, sautés them, and serves them with a warm mustard sauce. They are light and lush at the same time and definitely good enough to go to Philadelphia in search of (or you can buy Perrier's wonderful and accessible *Georges Perrier: Le Bec-Fin Recipes*).

My own favorite crab cake recipe came to me from the great and gifted book editor and equally gifted cook Jason Epstein. He can no longer remember where the recipe came from or even what it contains, but I can. I have been making these crab cakes regularly since the first time he made them for me, on my birthday, years ago. The crab is mixed with not much more than scallions, butter, and cream; the secret is the refrigeration. The cakes, when first formed, are almost runny, but they are immediately chilled until the butter and cream harden completely. Then they are quickly dipped in beaten egg, rolled in crumbs, and pan-fried. People always go crazy over these, and they can never figure out why they're so much better than other crab cakes. It's because by the time they are crisp and brown on the outside, nothing but pure crab is melting on the inside. They are so rich that I serve them with a tangy tomato vinaigrette, but small ones, passed as hors d'oeuvres, can be accompanied by traditional homemade tartar sauce.

Not that richness is necessarily a problem. When I was growing up, there was a famous restaurant in Memphis called Justine's. It was in a lovely old house, the flowers on the table were roses from the garden, and the thing everybody always ordered as a starter was Crabmeat Justine. Where I lived was about three hours away by car, but people would start talking about Crabmeat Justine, and the next thing you knew, somebody would volunteer to drive. I recently came across the recipe in an ancient copy of *The Memphis Cook Book*, published by the city's Junior League, and figured out why it was so incredibly good. It consists of only seasoned crabmeat sautéed in lemon and butter and topped with hollandaise sauce.

James Beard's favorite crab dish was Crab Louis, a recipe that originated on the Pacific coast, which means it was probably first made with Dungeness crab, but it is equally popular made with lumps of blue. The recipe appears in Beard's first cookbook, *Hors D'Oeuvres and Canapes*, and at least two subsequent ones, and he always played around a bit with the recipe (sometimes adding chopped green olives, sometimes using grated onion instead of chopped green onions). Beard insisted that the "finest" Louis he had ever had was at the Bohemian restaurant in his hometown, Portland, Oregon, though the recipe was served earlier by the chef at the Olympic Club in Seattle.

When the Metropolitan Opera touring company played that city in 1904, Enrico Caruso kept ordering the salad until none was left in the kitchen. It's too bad that Caruso didn't make it to New

Orleans, to Galatoire's, where the signature crab salad is Crab-meat Maison, a lump crab salad with mayonnaise, capers, and a bit of scallion. I love it on saltines topped with anchovies (a homey and weirdly delicious presentation made for me by my favorite waiter Richard), but at cocktail parties, I dress it up by serving it on toast points, without the anchovies. Once, at a particularly grand party, I filled an enormous silver punch bowl with about ten pounds of the stuff. It was so over the top that people sort of stood and stared at first, but within an hour it was gone.

Galatoire's is very big on crabmeat. If you ask them to, the wait-ers will top any fresh fish of the day with lumps that have been lightly sautéed in lemon and butter, and for serious crab lovers they will even pile it on top of soft-shells. They serve crabmeat hot, bound with a bit of béchamel and topped with bread crumbs and Parmesan in an appetizer known as Canapé Lorenzo, and cold, tossed into Godchaux Salad with boiled shrimp and Creole mus-tard vinaigrette topped with anchovies and hard-boiled eggs. How-ever, the best tossed salad featuring crabmeat is at another New Orleans institution, Mosca's, a roadhouse started by Provino Mosca, a favorite chef to the don of the New Orleans crime family, Carlos Marcello. Mosca's salad is simply iceberg lettuce, lump crabmeat, wine vinegar, olive oil, and an olivey antipasto salad (available by mail order from Central Grocery in New Orleans; 504-523-1620). Not long ago, I served it for lunch to a group of folks who included a French photographer, an English garden designer, a close friend of mine from Arkansas, and the photographer's assistant from Manhattan. None of them had ever tasted anything like it before, and none of them could get enough. You would have thought each was Caruso. They had discovered the curse of the crab—once you've had a taste, you must keep going back.

JASON'S BEST CRAB CAKES EVER

. . .

1½ sticks unsalted butter, plus 1 to 2 tablespoons for
   sautéing
1 cup finely chopped scallions (including some green tops)
½ cup finely chopped jalapeño pepper
¾ cup heavy cream
2 teaspoons Coleman's dry mustard
Pinch of cayenne pepper
2 pounds jumbo lump crabmeat, drained well, patted dry,
   picked over for shells
2 eggs, beaten
2 cups fresh, white bread crumbs, spread out in a baking
   dish
1 to 2 tablespoons vegetable oil

1. Melt 1½ sticks of butter in a large skillet over medium-high heat, add the scallions and jalapeño, and sauté for about 2 minutes, until bright green. Add the heavy cream and heat to boiling. Stir over medium heat 3 to 4 minutes, until the mixture thickens. Remove from the heat and stir in the dry mustard and cayenne. Cool 5 minutes.

2. Place the crabmeat in a large bowl. Gently stir in the scallion mixture. Form uniform cakes by placing spoonfuls of the crab mixture on a cookie sheet. Immediately place in refrigerator to harden, for about 2 hours.

3. When ready to serve, beat the eggs in a shallow bowl and place the bread crumbs in another shallow bowl. Melt 1 tablespoon

butter and 1 to 2 tablespoons oil in a large skillet over medium heat. Working with half of the crab cakes at a time (keep the remaining cakes in the refrigerator), dip each cake into the beaten eggs, then coat with crumbs. Sauté the crab cakes in the skillet until browned, 2 to 3 minutes on each side (turning the cakes only once, or they will break up). Drain the crab cakes on paper towels and serve immediately.

CRAB LOUIS

* * *

1 cup mayonnaise

¼ cup chili sauce

1 teaspoon Worcestershire
   sauce

¼ cup chopped green bell
   pepper

¼ cup chopped scallions

2 tablespoons fresh lemon
   juice

¼ cup heavy cream,
   whipped

Salt

Freshly ground black
   pepper

Cayenne pepper

6 cups shredded lettuce

3 cups jumbo lump
   crabmeat

3 ripe plum tomatoes,
   quartered

3 hard-boiled eggs,
   quartered

1. Combine the mayonnaise, chili sauce, Worcestershire, bell pepper, scallions, and lemon juice in a medium bowl and whisk until blended. Fold in the whipped cream and season to taste with the salt, black pepper, and cayenne.

2. Line a shallow salad bowl with shredded lettuce and mound the crabmeat on top. Spoon the dressing over the crab. Garnish with the tomatoes and hard-boiled eggs.

60 ⊙ Ham Biscuits, Hostess Gowns, and Other Southern Specialties

CRABMEAT JUSTINE

. . .

8 tablespoons (1 stick) unsalted butter

2 cups jumbo lump crabmeat

1 hard-boiled egg, grated

2 to 3 tablespoons fresh lemon juice

2 tablespoons dry sherry

Tabasco sauce

Four 5-inch warm toast squares, crusts removed

1¼ cups warm hollandaise sauce

1. Melt the butter in a large skillet over medium heat. Add the crabmeat, egg, lemon juice, sherry, and Tabasco to taste and stir until just heated through, being careful not to break up the lumps of crabmeat. (Make sure the mixture is well seasoned.)

2. Place the toast squares in individual 5-inch ramekins. Cover with the crabmeat and top with the hollandaise sauce.

3. Broil about 5 inches from heat for 3 to 5 minutes, until they are heated through and the tops are lightly browned. Serve immediately.

The Insider

❖

Most people remember their first raw oyster. "I swallowed once," wrote M.F.K. Fisher in *The Gastronomical Me*, "and felt light and attractive and daring, to know what I had done." Hers was at the Christmas banquet at the Southern California boarding school where she was a sophomore. Mine was at Doe's Eat Place in Greenville, Mississippi, where I grew up. "Try it," my father said, plopping an enormous Gulf oyster on my plate.

How could I not? I was the only child at the table, and my chief ambition was to somehow be thirty-five. I lifted the oyster out of its shell and swallowed it. First, there was the amazing surprise that the oyster was not in fact gross, but sweet and salty and actually good. ("Oysters, my delicate taste buds were telling me, oysters are *simply marvelous!*" Fisher wrote.) Then there was the breathtaking importance of the moment itself: I knew I had forever left the squeamish, fearful realm of childhood and become a risk-taking, experienced adult—despite the fact that I was only eleven.

Just as Fisher was downing her oyster, the senior-class president asked her to dance (an event made no less exciting by the fact that the president was also a girl). After I ate mine, I felt equally chosen, part of the "real" world I'd previously seen only in movies or at the edges of my parents' cocktail parties.

The good news is that the bright and sophisticated grown-up world, at least where oysters are concerned, is plenty large. I still eat oysters on the half shell every chance I get, but there are dozens of equally elegant ways to have them. There are angels on horseback (bacon-wrapped oysters broiled until the bacon is crisp), which were the height of cocktail party chic in the 50s and 60s, and which are still delicious, especially if you marinate the oysters first in white wine, garlic, and a little black pepper. There are Le Bernardin's sublime warm oysters anointed with black truffles and cream, a staple of the restaurant since its earliest days in Paris and a perfect combination of earth and sea. And then there are all those fabulous names: oysters casino, oysters Foch (pan-fried oysters atop toast smeared with a mousse of foie gras and topped with port-wine sauce), oysters Bienville (named for the founder of New Orleans and baked in their shells in a béchamel flavored with minced shrimp, garlic, and mushrooms, and topped with cheese), oysters poulette, oysters Pierre and, of course, oysters Rockefeller.

Oysters Rockefeller was invented at Antoine's Restaurant on St. Louis Street in New Orleans in 1899. The little black-and-gold book Antoine's published to celebrate its centennial in 1940 says that "Oysters à la Rockefeller . . . were so named because of the extreme richness of the sauce, because at the time the elder Rockefeller was then the richest man in the world." The family of Antoine Alciatore, which still owns the restaurant, has never divulged the recipe (on postcards printed to commemorate the millionth order, the recipe is referred to as "a sacred family secret"), but it is said to include an exotic mix of green herbs and watercress rather than the spinach with which the dish is so often made, and it is always flavored with either Pernod or anisette. I am firmly in the watercress camp, as was James Beard, who provided a recipe for it in his

New Fish Cookery. (Oysters topped with spinach are correctly called oysters Florentine, whose recipe is also in the book.) Among Beard's Rockefeller ingredients is fennel, which heightens the licorice flavor of the liqueur and is a strangely perfect match for oysters.

My Aunt Jane's favorite oyster dish was oysters Ellis; oysters baked on the half shell with chopped mushrooms and tomatoes and sauce Colbert. Aunt Jane smoked cigarettes out of a holder and wore rubies instead of diamonds, and her best friend killed her husband by running him through with a samurai sword. I'm pretty sure she ate oysters Ellis because they are delicious, not because she needed an aphrodisiac, as oysters are reputed to be. While there is something inherently sexy about eating an oyster, there is no scientific evidence that oysters themselves lift the libido. However, oyster loaves were once so successful in making up for the effects of the wandering male libido that they were called "peacemakers" in San Francisco and New Orleans, where errant husbands would bring them home to their furious brides in lieu of flowers or candy. (Aunt Jane's friend's husband should have tried this.) An oyster loaf is one of life's great things: a loaf of good French or homemade white bread, halved and hollowed out, brushed with butter, toasted, filled with fried oysters, and put back together again. Its particular elegance lies in its purity, but I have to admit that I find it hard not to spread the toasted bread cases with a film of tartar sauce made with homemade mayonnaise. It is better, perhaps, to save the tartar sauce for toasted rounds of a baguette, topped with a fried oyster, another great oyster canapé.

These days in New Orleans, the famous oyster loaves have mostly given way to oyster "po'boys," fried oysters on toasted—but not hollowed-out—French loaves and dressed with mayonnaise, lettuce, and tomato. There is an entire festival devoted to the glories of the po'boy in my adopted city, but I have never been much of a fan. The favored local "French" bread has the texture and taste of Styrofoam and it invariably gets in the way of the filling, which in the case of a properly fried oyster is a delicate thing. I much prefer the version at Casamento's, the Magazine Street oyster bar that opened in 1919. It is called an "oyster loaf" there, too, but it is made from a loaf of soft white, horizontally cut into thick slices, and toasted with butter. The bread doesn't fall apart and the oysters are perfectly fried and dressed and the whole thing is delicious. By the time it is brought to the Formica topped table (accompanied by homemade French fries when I am feeling especially deserving), I have usually consumed at least a dozen on the half shell. So far, at Casamento's alone, I have found three lovely pearls the size of map pin-heads. Tiles line the walls and a very happy fat cat lives just outside the screen door of the kitchen, through which you have to walk to get to the loo. It is here that I would take an oyster virgin for that first seminal experience. If she is very lucky, she will find a pearl, too. What could possibly make anyone feel more like a sophisticated citizen of the world?

OYSTERS ROCKEFELLER

Adapted from James Beard's New Fish Cookery

YIELD: 4 SERVINGS

. . .

8 tablespoons (1 stick)
  butter
¼ cup chopped fennel
  bulb
2 tablespoons chopped
  scallions
2 tablespoons chopped
  celery
1 tablespoon chopped fresh
  chervil
1 tablespoon chopped
  fennel greens
¼ cup chopped fresh flat-
  leaf parsley

1 cup trimmed fresh
  watercress, rinsed and
  dried
4 tablespoons fine, dry,
  plain bread crumbs
1 tablespoon Pernod or
  anisette liqueur,
  optional
½ teaspoon salt
¼ teaspoon freshly ground
  black pepper
Pinch of cayenne pepper
2 dozen oysters on the
  half shell

1. Preheat the oven to 475 degrees. Melt 3 tablespoons of the butter in a large nonstick skillet over medium-high heat and sauté the chopped fennel bulb, scallions, celery, chervil, fennel greens, and parsley for 3 minutes, or until tender. Add the watercress and cook 2 minutes, until just wilted. Place the mixture in a food processor. Add 3 tablespoons of butter, in pieces, 2 tablespoons bread crumbs, the Pernod, salt, black, and cayenne peppers. Process for 1 minute.

2. Arrange the oysters on a bed of rock salt in a shallow pan. Spread the fennel mixture on each. Melt the remaining 2 table-

spoons butter. Sprinkle the oysters with a pinch of bread crumbs and drizzle with the melted butter. Bake for 6 to 8 minutes, until the oysters are hot and plumped.

FRIED OYSTERS ROCKEFELLER SALAD

YIELD: 6 SERVINGS

. . .

FOR THE FRIED OYSTERS

1 cup yellow cornmeal

½ cup fine, dry bread crumbs from a loaf of French bread

1 teaspoon freshly ground black pepper

¼ teaspoon cayenne pepper

Salt

8 tablespoons butter (1 stick), melted

2 to 3 dozen oysters, shucked, drained, and dried on paper towels

Peanut or vegetable oil

FOR THE FENNEL AIOLI

2 medium fennel bulbs

1½ cups plus 3 tablespoons olive oil

1 tablespoon white wine vinegar

1½ teaspoons fennel seeds, chopped

3 garlic cloves, peeled and sliced

3 large egg yolks

Salt and white pepper

FOR THE SALAD

2½ tablespoons fresh lemon juice

Two 3-inch strips lemon peel, minced

¾ teaspoon salt

¼ teaspoon freshly ground black pepper

⅛ teaspoon fennel seeds, crushed under a spoon or chopped

4 to 5 teaspoons extra-
virgin olive oil

2 bunches watercress,
trimmed, rinsed, and
dried

1 bunch flat-leaf parsley,
rinsed and dried; stems
removed

½ cup thinly sliced celery

2 tablespoons minced
fennel greens

2 tablespoons chopped
fresh chervil

2 tablespoons chopped
fresh chives

1 loaf of French bread,
thinly sliced, brushed
with olive oil, and
toasted (about 30
slices)

Fennel aioli

2½ dozen fried oysters

To prepare the oysters: Mix the cornmeal with the bread crumbs and seasonings and put in a shallow pan.

Dip the oysters in the melted butter and then in the cornmeal mixture to coat, and place them on a cookie sheet.

Heat 1 inch of oil in a heavy skillet over medium heat until the temperature reaches 375 degrees, or until a piece of bread dropped in the pan sizzles. Place the oysters in the skillet a few at a time and fry until golden brown, no more than 2 minutes, turning once. Before adding more, wait for the oil to come back to temperature.

Drain the cooked oysters on paper towels and taste for more salt. Repeat until all the oysters are fried, adding more oil as needed.

To make the aioli: Trim the fennel bulbs and cut into thin slices. Heat the 3 tablespoons of oil in a skillet over medium heat. Add the fennel slices, vinegar, and seeds and sauté for 10 minutes, stirring often. Add 1½ garlic cloves and the remaining oil. Reduce the heat to low, cover, and cook until the fennel is tender, stirring occasionally, about 35 minutes.

Remove the fennel and garlic mixture to a food processor, reserving the oil. (Do not use a blender.) Add the remaining garlic to the food processor. Puree. With the machine running, add the egg yolks one at a time, and process until smooth.

Gradually add the oil from the fennel mixture in a slow, steady stream, while the machine is running. Process until emulsified. Season with salt and white pepper to taste.

NOTE: This makes about 2 cups and is also terrific with shrimp or any poached white fish.

To assemble the salad: Mix the lemon juice, lemon peel, salt, pepper, and fennel seeds in a large bowl. Slowly whisk in the oil to make a vinaigrette.

Add the watercress, parsley, celery, fennel greens, chervil, and chives. Toss until coated.

Place a tangle of greens on each of six large plates. Spread four to five slices of toast with fennel aioli and top each with a fried oyster. Place in a circle around the salad.

Prep School

❁

My mother is a superlative human being and gives the best dinner parties of anyone I know, but she has a small problem with time. In her long and rich life as a hostess, for example, she has never, not once, greeted her guests at the door. By now they have come to expect it. They accept drinks from my father and are always happy to see her when she finally emerges. They know that she's not being rude—she is simply in the bathtub.

Sadly, this seems to be a hereditary trait. I've usually made it out of the bath when my guests arrive, but just barely. (Once, wrapped only in a towel, I opened the door to a very prompt and highly embarrassed male guest because I thought it was the ice man, and he's used to seeing me in disarray.) And then, as soon as I'm done hugging and kissing and bartending, I'm back in the kitchen again, finishing sauces, assembling (or, alas, cooking) the first course, checking on dessert. When I finally get to the table, I am so exhausted and stressed out and relieved, all I want to do is suck down the nearest bottle of wine. There is no excuse for this, really, because with a little organization it is possible, even without any staff, to prepare an entire dinner ahead of time, enjoy cocktails with your guests, and have no need to get completely smashed upon sitting down.

In the winter this goal is especially easy. I make a daube or a stew a day or two ahead of time (either one is always better after it sits anyway), reheat it, and bring it out with French bread and a green salad. In the summer, I'll serve a cold tenderloin or a poached salmon or a vitello tonnato, all of which can be made at least a day ahead. But it is also possible to achieve a more formal meal. To this end, lately I have been making a lot of rib-eye roasts. There is nothing easier or more delicious—simply preheat the oven to 500 degrees, rub a boneless rib roast with lots of butter and salt and pepper, and cook exactly five minutes per pound. Then turn the oven off, but don't open the door, and leave the meat inside for another hour and a half. It will be crusty on the outside and a perfect rare to medium-rare on the inside, and the entire amount of prep work is less than five minutes.

Everything else can be made the night before. A potato gratin would be a perfect accompaniment or Wolfgang Puck's beautiful and delicious carrot loaf. I also love the recipe for squash gratin my friend M.T. got from Lydie Marshall, whose cooking school she regularly attends in the south of France. M.T., who for years produced miracles out of a Manhattan kitchen the size of a postage stamp, had no choice but to cook everything well ahead of the appointed hour. She only had room enough to cook one item at a time.

M.T. and I cook really well together—she is efficient and I am a tad grandiose and messy, and somehow it all works perfectly. One of our more memorable efforts was a Mardi Gras dinner party I decided to give in New York. It was impromptu, so we had not prepared much of anything in advance, but it was one of those nights when we were happy to have a reason to avoid the living room. We made an enormous feast of shrimp rémoulade and oysters Rockefeller and chicken étouffée and bread pudding (all of which we could have easily made earlier, including the Rockefeller sauce). The food was really good, but somehow I had assembled an unusually toxic mix of people. When we went to the kitchen to put the shrimp on a platter, we closed the door so we could talk about how obnoxious everybody was acting, and when we tried to open it, it was stuck. You have never seen two happier girls. We didn't scream for help or bang on anything; we just opened the window and smoked, and hoped that no one would ever find us.

They did, of course, which in that particular case was too bad, but it was the exception, not the rule. Usually, I am happy to see my friends. And very happy to sit down with them without a splattered blouse or hair wilted from heat and effort, to hear complete conversations rather than tantalizing snippets on my way in and out of the room. Also, when the hostess is constantly in the kitchen, the guests invariably feel compelled to come and "lend a hand," and there is actually nothing less helpful. So, I am working on being a serene, together hostess, one who is made up and well dressed (I am invariably the worst-dressed person at my own parties, because I leave myself about thirty seconds to pull something over my head), one who answers her own door, mingles through cocktails, and dazzles the crowd with complicated-seeming, individual pudding soufflés that she has in fact made a whole day ahead of time. And then I'm going to give the recipe to my mother.

CARROT LOAF

Adapted from Modern French Cooking for the American Kitchen,
by Wolfgang Puck

YIELD: 8 SERVINGS

. . .

12 tablespoons (1½ sticks) unsalted butter

2 pounds carrots, peeled and cut into ¼-inch slices

¼ pound mushrooms, cut into ¼-inch slices

1 pound fresh spinach, rinsed well and dried (if you are
    not using baby spinach, remove the stems)

6 eggs

1 cup grated Gruyère or Swiss cheese (4 ounces)

1 teaspoon salt

1 teaspoon freshly ground pepper

Melt 4 tablespoons of the butter in a large skillet over medium heat. Add the carrots and sauté slowly until tender, about 25 minutes. Chop coarsely and place in a bowl.

Increase the heat to high and melt 2 tablespoons of the butter in the same skillet. Add the mushrooms and sauté for 2 minutes. Chop coarsely and add to the carrots. Set aside.

Melt 4 tablespoons of the butter over medium-high heat in the same skillet, add the spinach, and sauté until wilted, about 2 minutes. Chop coarsely, place in a separate bowl, and set aside.

Line an 8½× 4½× 2½-inch loaf pan with aluminum foil. Butter the foil with the remaining 2 tablespoons of butter. Beat together 4 eggs, the cheese, salt, and pepper in a medium bowl, add to the carrot mixture, and mix well. Spread half the carrot mixture over the bottom of the pan, cover with the spinach mixture, and top with the remaining carrot mixture. Cover the loaf with plastic wrap and refrigerate (the loaf may be prepared and refrigerated for up to a day ahead of time).

Preheat the oven to 400 degrees. Remove the plastic wrap from the loaf pan, cover loosely with aluminum foil, and place in a roasting pan. Add enough boiling water to come halfway up the sides of the pan. Bake for 1 hour, or until a knife plunged in the center comes out clean. Uncover, invert the loaf onto a serving platter, and remove the foil. Slice and serve immediately.

CHEESE PUDDING SOUFFLÉS

YIELD: 6 SERVINGS

* * *

4 tablespoons butter

¼ cup all-purpose flour

1½ cups milk, slightly warmed

1 teaspoon salt

2 sprigs fresh thyme

1 medium onion, diced

½ cup scallions, including a bit of the green part, thinly sliced

½ cup garlic cloves, peeled and thinly sliced

Pinch of cayenne

½ cup grated Gruyère cheese (about 2 ounces)

½ teaspoon freshly ground black pepper

3 large eggs, separated

⅓ cup heavy cream

Melt 3 tablespoons of the butter over medium-low heat. Add the flour and cook for a few minutes, stirring constantly. Pour in the milk a little at a time, whisking after each addition until smooth. Add ½ teaspoon salt and the thyme sprigs. Reduce the heat to very low and cook, stirring frequently, until the sauce is medium-thick, about 20 minutes. Let cool to room temperature and remove the thyme sprigs.

Melt the remaining tablespoon of butter in a skillet over medium heat and cook the onion until translucent, about 5 minutes. Add the scallions, garlic, ½ teaspoon salt, and ¼ cup water. Reduce the heat and cook until the garlic is soft and the water has nearly evaporated, about 10 minutes; add more water if necessary to keep the vegetables from browning. Set aside to cool.

Puree the mixture in a food processor, add the sauce, cayenne, Gruyère, and ½ teaspoon pepper and process until blended. Taste and adjust the seasoning—it should be fairly highly seasoned. Add the egg yolks and process until blended. Transfer the mixture to a large bowl.

Preheat the oven to 400 degrees. Generously butter six 6-ounce ramekins or custard cups. Beat the egg whites in a medium bowl until they form soft peaks and gently fold them into the cheese mixture. (Do not overfold.) Spoon the soufflé mixture into the ramekins and place them in a baking pan. Add enough boiling water to come halfway up the sides of the molds. Bake until the soufflés are puffed and a light golden brown, 20 to 30 minutes.

Carefully remove the ramekins. When the soufflés have cooled a bit, unmold them by running a paring knife around the edges, inverting each soufflé into the palm of your hand, and placing it in a shallow baking dish, top side up. They can now be held at room temperature for a few hours. They can also be held in the refrigerator, covered in plastic wrap, overnight.

When ready to serve, preheat the oven to 425 degrees. If refrigerated, bring the soufflés to room temperature. Pour the cream over and around the soufflés. Bake until the cream is hot and bubbling and the soufflés are puffed up again, about 6 to 8 minutes. Serve with the hot cream.

SQUASH-AND-ONION GRATIN

Adapted from Chez Nous: Home Cooking from the South of France,
by Lydie Marshall

YIELD: 6 TO 8 SERVINGS

◦ ◦ ◦

5 pounds zucchini, or a mix of zucchini and yellow squash,
    cut into ½-inch slices
4 large onions, thinly sliced
1½ cups grated Gruyère cheese (about 6 ounces)
1 cup ricotta cheese
2 large garlic cloves, minced
1½ teaspoons salt
Freshly ground black pepper

Combine the zucchini and onions in a large stockpot. Cover
with water and boil until the vegetables are tender, about 30 minutes. Drain in a colander, pushing firmly to extract all the liquid.

Combine the Gruyère, ricotta, garlic, salt, and pepper. Add the
vegetables, mix well, and taste and adjust the seasonings. Butter a
3-quart casserole and fill with the squash mixture. Cover with plastic wrap and refrigerate until ready to cook.

Preheat the oven to 400 degrees. Uncover the casserole and
bake on the middle shelf until golden brown and bubbly, about 30
minutes.

Hostess Cupcakes

❖

The first thing that should be said about hostess gowns is that it is not, in fact, proper to use the term at all. In *Vogue's Book of Etiquette*, a still mostly invaluable guide published in 1948, readers are instructed that "hostess-gown should not be used for 'tea gown,'" just as "there is absolutely no excuse for a commercial word such as 'hosiery' in normal conversation" ("Stockings" is preferred). And, my favorite, "there is almost no permissible simile" for the description "high-toned" at all. (You may substitute "smart," Vogue tells us, but "the best mental usage would omit the whole idea.")

A lot, of course, has changed since 1948. For one thing, Millicent Fenwick, the *Vogue* editor who authored the book, went on to become a member of Congress from New Jersey, and, presumably, concerned herself with more important issues than the relative vulgarity of "hostess gown" compared to "tea gown." And for another, by any name, these frocks, specifically designed for entertaining at home, are not much worn anymore.

This is a shame, for there are few garments quite so glamorous. The original hostess gowns (we are going to ignore Millicent here) were sort of elaborate dressing gowns—with a bodice that was buttoned or wrapped tightly, cinched at the waist with a wide sash or crushed belt, and featuring a full skirt either flowing to the ground or ankle length, worn with ballet flats or mules. Joan Bennett, the actress and mother of my friend Shelley Wanger, wore them almost every night, even to dinner with her children. Bennett was gorgeous (a word the *Vogue* book says should be applied only to sunsets and highly colored objects), and her hostess gowns were, too. "They were always in evening fabrics," Wanger tells me. There was one in gold lamé, for example, and others with big cuffs worn with cuff links. "And she wore them with open-toed satin mules, which had pom-poms made of satin rope."

My friend M.T.'s grandmother Mary Alma had one in heavy gold brocade. "The skirt was big, and it totally swung out," says M.T., who thinks she wore it with matching gold mules. I don't remember the shoes, either, but I can tell you what she would have served when she wore it: asparagus roll-ups—slices of white bread pounded thin, brushed with melted butter, sprinkled with grated Parmesan and cayenne pepper, and rolled around blanched asparagus spears, placed on cookie sheets and shoved briefly in the oven. Like the gown, the recipe was one of her signatures, and when I gave my first cocktail party, I got it from her—though, sadly I did not have a gown for the occasion. Those were the days when women entertained all the time and had a vast repertoire of things (most often wrapped up in other things) to pass around: oysters, dates, or water chestnuts wrapped in bacon and broiled; olives covered with cheese pastry (though they're mighty good wrapped in bacon, too); grapes covered in blue cheese and rolled in crushed pecans; "pigs" encased in their puff pastry blankets; and another of Mary Alma's mainstays, sweet pickles encased in cream cheese, rolled in a thin piece of ham, and sliced, for the full pink-and-green pinwheel effect.

The hors d'oeuvres that weren't passed were served from chafing dishes. Our dining room table always had a minimum of two going, one with some kind of creamy hot seafood accompanied by toast points and another with a cheesy, spicy spinach dip my mother called spinach madrilene. By then, hostess gowns had morphed a bit into the long full wrap skirts my mother wore with fitted satin blouses—red satin with a gold-and-red wool skirt for the holidays; black satin with a gold-and-black-and-cream skirt for other times. Though I was still in elementary school I had some, too. My grandmother frequently forgot I was a child and bought me the same clothes she bought my mother. So when my parents entertained their friends, I entertained their children, holding court in the playroom, pouring sparkling Catawba grape juice instead of champagne (though, thrillingly, the bottle looked exactly the same) for Amanda and McGee and Elizabeth and Meta, for M.T. and Cordelia and Robert and William. One Christmas I was given a long skirt in black-and-red-and-green plaid, which I wore with a white ruffled poet's blouse that I wish I still had; on another, I got pants and a tunic made of pale blue angora shot through with silver Lurex—a brilliant at-home ensemble that I nonetheless insisted on showing off to my fifth-grade class as soon as the holidays were over.

My mother wore pants, too, wide-legged numbers as full as her skirts, but sexier somehow, more swish. These were called palazzo pants, perhaps because they were meant for entertaining in your own private palazzo. (The dictionary defines *palazzo* as any imposing structure, so the name could also derive from the ample size of the pant leg.) In one memorable episode of *I Love Lucy*, these pants were referred to outright as "hostess pants" when Lucy suggests to Fred that he give a pair to Ethel for her birthday. Ethel, not surprisingly, doesn't have any idea what they are. "They're hostess pants; you wear them when you throw smart dinner parties," Lucy explains to her unconvinced friend, who shoots back that she "was wondering what to wear to all those smart dinner parties I throw." Lucy forges ahead, explaining, "You get yourself a little off-the-shoulder blouse, a big crushy belt and ballet slippers, and you're all set," at which point Ethel says: "For what? Halloween?"

It's true that such an ensemble probably wouldn't have looked all that great on Ethel, though it would've been perfect for Lucy, whom I can picture wearing it with some oversized hoop or chandelier earrings. Lucy, or Lucille Ball, wore a version of hostess pants, in voluminous red jersey with a batwinged top, in the opening party scene of *Mame*, one of the worst movie musicals ever made. The film was set in the 1920s and 30s, but the outfit was exactly like the hostess frocks my mother had started wearing by the 70s, brightly colored jersey caftans and gowns by Stephen Burrows and Clovis Ruffin. I have a picture of her in one, black, to the floor, covered in multicolored stars. She had on huge Kenneth Jay Lane gold and lapis hoops and she was smoking a Salem.

These days it is possible to buy hostessy attire, but I want the real deal, the wrapped gown with the big skirt in a half dozen different colors and fabrics and low-heeled Manolo mules to match. It's the perfect ensemble for hurried and harried hostesses like me, who, after fussing over food and flowers, tend to reach for the nearest thing in the closet before running to get the door. How much easier—and chicer—to simply wrap a gown around myself, step into my jeweled mules, and make a grand entrance down the stairs. And how much chicer still to be carrying a silver tray of delicious stuffed olives in cheese pastry.

So, I propose a return to the days when women took entertaining to such professional heights they had their own uniforms. To the days when mothers like Joan Bennett donned hostess attire even when their only guests were their own families. I am not talking about the kind of tortured, once-a-year entertaining like the party Julianne Moore throws in *Far from Heaven*, with the teal tablecloths and the endless consultations with the caterers. No wonder Dennis Quaid got soused. I want a rack of gowns—or pants or skirts—in my closet and a stack of cookie sheets (and at least one chafing dish) in my kitchen so that I can switch effortlessly into hostess mode any time somebody drops in for a highball and a roll-up. For once, I want to be the most glamorous woman at my own party.

HOT CHEESE OLIVES

YIELD: 50 HORS D OEUVRES

. . .

8 tablespoons (1 stick) butter, softened

8 ounces (2 cups) grated extra-sharp cheddar cheese

1½ cups unsifted all-purpose flour

⅛ teaspoon salt

¼ teaspoon cayenne pepper

Dash of Worcestershire sauce

1 large egg

50 small pimento-stuffed cocktail olives, drained and
    patted dry

Preheat the oven to 350 degrees. Beat the butter until creamy in a large mixing bowl, add the cheese, and mix well. Stir in the flour, salt, cayenne, and Worcestershire until smooth. Beat the egg with 2 tablespoons of cold water. Add to the dough and mix just until incorporated. Refrigerate for 30 minutes.

Remove the dough and flatten out a piece about the size of a walnut into a thin round. Place an olive on top and shape it around the olive, pinching to repair any breaks. Place it on an ungreased cookie sheet. Repeat with the remaining dough and olives. Bake until the dough sets, about 15 minutes. Serve hot.

CRABMEAT MORNAY

Adapted from Bayou Cuisine

YIELD: 10 TO 12 SERVINGS

. . .

8 tablespoons (1 stick) butter, softened

1 bunch scallions, chopped, with some green tops included

2 tablespoons all-purpose flour

2 cups heavy cream

8 ounces (about 2 cups) grated Gruyère or Swiss cheese

1 tablespoon dry sherry

¼ teaspoon cayenne pepper

¼ teaspoon salt

1 pound jumbo lump crabmeat

½ cup chopped flat-leaf parsley

Toast points or tart shells (Siljans is a good, crispy brand)

Melt the butter in a heavy saucepan over medium-high heat. Add the scallions and sauté for about 3 minutes until soft.

Whisk in the flour. Add the cream and whisk until smooth. Stir in the grated cheese and blend until smooth. Add the sherry and cayenne and ¼ teaspoon salt (or more to taste), and gently fold in the crabmeat and chopped parsley.

Serve in a chafing dish accompanied by toast points, or fill small tart shells and pass them on trays.

A Fan's Notes

❖

I did not have an upbringing that was remotely oriented toward football. I don't think I ever saw my father watch a game on TV. (Though I know he used to bet on them—everybody did. Until he was busted, the owner of a popular café downtown was also a bookie.) When I left home, it was to go to an all-girls boarding school (where I saw a hockey stick for the first time but not, obviously, a football) and then to Georgetown, where basketball was the thing. (Patrick Ewing arrived my sophomore year.) I did give a Super Bowl party once, but even that was accidental—I invited people over for dinner one Sunday, and they all pointed out that the game would be on. Deflated, I bought a bucket of Popeyes Fried Chicken, made a pot of gumbo, and perked up only during the commercials.

But all that changed on a sunny October Saturday a few years back when I watched Ole Miss stomp the hell out of Alabama. I am a person of easy enthusiasms, and this conversion was especially easy for several reasons. One, the game was so good that I could follow what was going on despite my extreme lack of knowledge. It was the last college season of Eli Manning, who threw a particularly dazzling pass in midstride, and the team scored twenty-four points in the first quarter. Two, Eli is adorable and by all accounts a really good guy, as are his father, Archie, former Ole Miss and New Orleans Saints quarterback (who also happens to be my neighbor), and his brothers, Cooper and Peyton, the quarterback for the Indianapolis Colts. Peyton watched his brother from the sidelines that day surrounded by a virtual platoon of state troopers (who looked as if they just wanted to be there rather than as if they were actually needed to protect him). I watched him through binoculars and don't think I've ever seen someone concentrate on the action before him with such laserlike intensity. Thoroughly smitten, my pro-football allegiances became immediately determined by the affiliations of the Manning brothers. (As most of the civilized world now knows, Eli went on to become quarterback for the New York Giants and Ole Miss has been suffering ever since.)

I have to admit, however, that the most likely reason for my newfound love of the game was the extremely plush surroundings in which I watched it. Several years ago, Ole Miss made some improvements to its stadium, including thirty swanky new boxes that were made available to its most loyal alums and other assorted high rollers, for $250,000 for a thirteen-year lease. My good friend the artist Bill Dunlap got me invited to one owned by a very gracious couple from Jackson, and it boasted a huge powder room, delicious hors d'oeuvres, maid service, and an enormous (and stunning, of course) Dunlap landscape hanging on the wall. There was a full bar featuring excellent Bloody Marys and a long buffet, where I ate some delicious barbecue and someone's yummy birthday cake. It was a gorgeous, barely crisp fall day, and everybody was really, really happy, and I decided that life was grand and that America was a wonderful country.

With this in mind, I have decided to nurture my fledgling fanhood by creating festive, slightly high-toned environments whenever a big game is on TV, starting, naturally, with the Super Bowl. There is no reason that Super Bowl parties have to take place in rooms littered with crushed Fritos and bad bean dip. For example, in *Alfred Portale's 12 Season Cookbook,* the fine chef-owner of the Gotham Bar and Grill offers up two Super Bowl menus. One includes a black bean soup with tomato-avocado salsa, slow-cooked lamb shoulder (a recipe that alone is worth the price of the cookbook), and a decadent-sounding peanut butter *coupe* made from chocolate sorbet, chocolate sauce, praline ice cream, peanuts, and peanut butter.

I must say that I was surprised to run across any mention of the Super Bowl in Portale's book, where the other menus include one for New Year's featuring foie gras with cherry chutney and an all-French one with delicious salmon rillettes, but he's from Buffalo, he roots for the Bills, and every year he gives a Super Bowl party for his staff at the restaurant, complete with wide-screen TVs. He explains that they are so busy during the holidays that there is no time for a Christmas bash, so the game is "our way of sneaking in one last holiday gathering long after the official season has come and gone." They even put on their own halftime show—one year a waiter dressed in drag and serenaded Portale's hometown team.

The entertainment opportunities similar to those at Portale's parties have further encouraged my devotion to the game. I may not have grown up with rabid football fans, but I do come from a long line of people who like to put on pageants and plays and generally entertain one another. In the past, when LSU has been invited to play in the Sugar Bowl, I have kept up with the score largely by listening to my husband's cheers—I am almost always in the next room glue-gunning a tiara to wear to the annual masked costume ball that takes place a few days later. The ball is the kind of event I have historically been more partial to. But thanks to Portale's inspiration, I can combine my old passion with my new— next year I am going to give a big bash complete with an elaborate halftime show.

No matter what happens, it will be easy to raise the bar on what is considered proper "football food." The recipe for the black-bean-and-pork stew is a nod to the inevitable salsa-and-chips that are staples of most Super Bowl parties (it should be served with home-made salsa cruda and warm flour tortillas), and its spiciness should introduce some zip into what I'm told are usually rather bland championship games. The Carbonnade Flamande, a Belgian stew made with beef and onions, is a nod to the fact that the Super Bowl is traditionally a big beer night. I make and serve the carbonnade with the Czech Pilsner Urquell or the Belgian Duvel, which, with 8.5 percent alcohol, packs quite a punch. With the pork stew, I'd recommend a Mexican lager like Bohemia or the dark Negra Modelo. You might also serve Young's Double Chocolate Stout, made by the oldest brewery in England, which has a taste that goes surprisingly well with both dishes.

PORK STEW WITH BLACK BEANS

Adapted from The Feast of Santa Fe, *by Huntley Dent*

YIELD: 8 SERVINGS

- 2 cups dried black beans
- 1 teaspoon salt, plus more to taste
- 2 bay leaves
- 1 teaspoon dried oregano
- 1 teaspoon freshly ground black pepper
- 1 teaspoon whole cumin seed
- 6 jalapeño peppers, seeded and deveined
- 4 garlic cloves, peeled
- 2 onions, cut into rough chunks
- 2 tablespoons cayenne pepper
- 4 tablespoons sweet paprika, preferably Spanish or Hungarian
- 4 tablespoons cornmeal
- 4 tablespoons vegetable oil
- 3 pounds boneless pork shoulder, trimmed and cut into ½-inch cubes
- 4 tablespoons honey
- 2 teaspoons ground cumin
- 2 teaspoons ground cinnamon
- Cooked rice for serving

Wash and drain the beans several times. Place in a large pot with 8 cups water, 1 teaspoon salt, and the bay leaves, oregano, black pepper, and cumin seed. Cover, but keep the lid slightly ajar, and boil until tender, about 2 hours, stirring occasionally and adding more water if needed to keep the beans covered. Drain the beans and reserve the cooking liquid.

Pulse the jalapeños and garlic in a food processor; add the onions and pulse again. Remove and set aside.

Add the cayenne, paprika, and cornmeal to the food processor.

While processing, pour in about 1 cup of the reserved cooking liquid from the beans to make a smooth paste.

Heat the oil in a heavy 6-quart pot. Brown the pork cubes in 4 to 5 batches over medium-high heat, removing the cubes as they brown. When the last batch is browned, add the other pork cubes and their juices and the honey, ground cumin, and cinnamon. Stir to scrape up any brown bits from the bottom of the pan.

Lower the heat and add the onion mixture. Cook, stirring, until heated through, then add the cornmeal paste and 4 cups of the reserved bean cooking liquid (if there is not enough, add some water) and stir. Bring to a simmer, cover, and simmer for 30 minutes, stirring frequently to keep the mixture from sticking. Add the beans and salt to taste, stir, and simmer another 30 minutes. Serve over rice.

CARBONNADE A LA FLAMANDE

3 pounds rump or chuck roast, cut into 2-inch cubes

3 tablespoons bacon fat, or a mixture of butter and olive oil, or more if necessary

Salt

Freshly ground black pepper

6 cups sliced yellow onions (about 1½ pounds)

4 garlic cloves, pressed

1 cup beef stock

2 to 3 cups beer

2 tablespoons brown sugar

1 herb bouquet (6 parsley sprigs, 4 thyme branches, and 1 bay leaf tied together)

1½ tablespoons arrowroot or cornstarch

2 tablespoons red wine vinegar

Buttered noodles for serving

Place a rack in the lower third of the oven. Preheat the oven to 325 degrees. Dry the beef and heat the fat in a 9- to 10-inch oven-proof casserole or pot until almost smoking. Brown the beef quickly on all sides, a few pieces at a time, removing them as they brown. Sprinkle with salt and pepper, toss to season evenly, and set aside.

Reduce the heat. Stir in the onions, adding more fat if necessary. Brown lightly, about 10 minutes, stirring frequently. Season with salt and pepper to taste. Stir in the garlic. Set aside. Add the stock to the pan and scrape up the brown bits and coagulated juices.

Arrange half the beef in the pan and spread with half the

onions. Repeat with the remaining beef and onions. Add enough beer to cover the meat. Stir in the brown sugar and bury the herb bouquet in the meat. Bring to a simmer, cover, and place in the oven. Cook at a slow simmer (check occasionally) for 2½ hours, or until the meat is tender.

Remove the casserole from the oven and discard the herb bouquet. Remove the beef, and skim off the fat from the liquid. Blend the arrowroot with the vinegar and stir into the liquid in the casserole. Simmer for 3 to 4 minutes, until thickened. Taste and adjust the seasonings. Return the meat to the casserole, stir, and heat through. Serve with buttered noodles.

Bighearted Shrimp

❖

It is irritating to me that the word "shrimp," when not applied to the long-tailed crustacean of the genus *Crangon*, means "a small or unimportant person," (*The American Heritage Dictionary*), "a very small slight person" (*The Oxford Desk Dictionary*), and "a diminutive or puny person . . . chiefly *contemptuous*" (*The Oxford English Dictionary*). Worse, according to the O.E.D., the term *shrimp-hearted* means cowardly, and *to shrimp*, in addition to fishing for same, means to suck someone's toes (though the latter definition is not found in any of my dictionaries).

This is an unfair and terrible fate to befall the majestic and extremely delicious shrimp. To me, shrimp is the ur-seafood—to eat it is to taste the very essence of the ocean. It is an excellent source of animal protein, not nearly as expensive or hard to get at as lobster or crabmeat, and far more versatile in cooking. (My seafood bible, *James Beard's New Fish Cookery*, contains fifty recipes for shrimp, compared with thirty-seven for lobster, eighteen for crab, and four for crawfish.) It's beautiful, too: the O.E.D. lists another definition as the "bright shade of pink" the shrimp turns when cooked.

Undeterred by the shrimp's derogatory connotations, Americans eat more of it than any other shellfish. The great majority is imported from places like Ecuador and China, and most of that is farm-raised. When a fishmonger tells you his shrimp is "fresh," he usually means that it has only recently been thawed, which is fine, because shrimp freezes well. In Manhattan, the buyer at my old neighborhood fish market told me a few years ago that he "easily" sold 300 pounds of shrimp a week, mostly frozen, from Ecuador and Panama. But, he added, he bought fresh Gulf shrimp flown in from Florida whenever he could, as he had several customers with standing orders.

I don't blame them. I'll eat shrimp any way I can get it, but fresh Gulf shrimp, and fresh shrimp from the coast of the Carolinas and northern Georgia are superior delicacies. I like to buy shrimp fresh off the boat, wrapped in newspaper and rushed to the nearest stove. When shrimp are that fresh, the best way to prepare them is to peel them and sauté them in butter or to boil them with their shells on in salted, seasoned water. Beard wrote that "the unpardonable fault in preparing shrimp is overcooking." You want to cook shrimp just long enough to give them some firmness and color; you do not want to achieve the Super Ball consistency that marked the shrimp cocktails of my youth.

There's a lot of conversation about the best way to boil shrimp, and much has been made of the method of adding shrimp to boiling water, bringing it back to a boil, immediately turning off the fire, and letting the shrimp sit for five minutes, or even until the water cools. Don't do it! For one to four pounds of shrimp, boil three quarts of water with three tablespoons of salt, a couple of quartered lemons, and a bag of Zatarain's Crawfish, Shrimp, and Crab Boil (available at www.zatarains.com). Boil for about ten minutes, add the shrimp, and check after two minutes. Unless the shrimp are very large, they will probably be done. (Remember they will continue cooking in their shells for a bit even after they're drained.) Remove the pot from the heat and dump the shrimp into a colander.

In New Orleans, boiled gulf shrimp is almost always served with sauce rémoulade. And when it's sautéed, it's usually paired with other ingredients and given swanky names like Shrimp Clemenceau (with cubed potatoes, mushrooms, and peas) or Shrimp Yvonne (with mushrooms and sliced artichoke hearts). The sautéed shrimp of the low country has traditionally been a more straightforward affair, cooked in butter or bacon grease and served with grits at breakfast. These days "breakfast shrimp" and grits is a dish no longer confined to the private kitchens of Beaufort and Savannah—or to the first meal of the day. Variations of the classic combo are now found on lunch and dinner menus across the country, thanks largely to the late, great Bill Neal and to Donald Barickman, who almost twenty years ago put a version with tasso (a highly seasoned, cured ham) gravy on the menu at Magnolia's in Charleston. I also have had a superb version, a highly seasoned, creamy concoction with chunks of tomatoes, at a delightful restaurant, Pearl's Café, in landlocked Sewanee, Tennessee.

That dish, which I've tried to replicate here, is much like what New Orleanians call Shrimp Cardinale, which is usually served in a ramekin and never, ever with something as low class as grits. Unlike the English and Huguenot Carolinas, New Orleans was Latin and cosmopolitan, a city of restaurants; country fare like grits never really took hold. It is only now that shrimp and grits has been deemed cool that it has shown up on menus. The best version is at Joanne Clevenger's fabulous Upperline. Clevenger, who is from central Louisiana, has had much success in melding the down-home foods of her youth with more sophisticated city fare. She is famous as the inventor of the Original Fried Green Tomato with Shrimp Rémoulade.

Now she and chef Kenneth Smith have another hit with Cane River Country Shrimp. It consists of shrimp with lots of garlic, Tabasco, mushrooms, and bacon sautéed and deglazed with cream and finished with shrimp bisque. It is served over squares of fried grits. The mushrooms are a nod to Clemenceau and Yvonne; the bacon, a nod to the low country. "The waiters tell me that when people hear about the bacon, they perk up," Smith says.

Another classic way to prepare shrimp is to fry it. I have found the holy grail of fried shrimp (well, actually, the holy trinity, since I have found it in three places) at Captain Benny's Half-Shell Oyster Bar in Houston, Texas; The Shrimp Shack in Beaufort, South Carolina; and Doe's Eat Place in Greenville, Mississippi. I've learned not to mess with perfection, so when I "fry" shrimp, it is in the form of fritters. There is a particularly wonderful "fritter" from the southern coast of Spain, called *tortillitas de camarones*. *Camarones* are tiny shrimp found off Cádiz and dropped live into a simple batter. I learned to love them—and to make them—in a bar called El Paseillo in Madrid, a short walk from the bull ring. The owner's wife grew up in San Fernando, in Cádiz, and she makes the only non-greasy version I've ever had. (The trick, she says, is to spread the batter into an almost lacy consistency once it's in the oil; otherwise the *tortillitas* take too long to cook and absorb too much grease.) These are easily replicated here by chopping shrimp finely and make excellent hot hors d'oeuvres.

SHRIMP AND GRITS

YIELD: 4 SERVINGS

* * *

FOR THE GRITS

¾ cup grits

¼ teaspoon salt

6 ounces white cheddar cheese, grated (or a mixture of
    half cheddar, half Parmesan)

3 tablespoons butter

FOR THE SHRIMP

4 tablespoons butter

¾ cup chopped onion

½ cup chopped green bell
    pepper

2 garlic cloves, minced

1 cup diced ripe tomatoes
    with a little of their
    juice (chopped canned
    tomatoes are preferable
    to less-than-perfect
    fresh tomatoes)

½ teaspoon dried thyme

1 tablespoon all-purpose
    flour

1 pound medium to large
    raw shrimp, shelled
    (reserve the shells for
    stock)

½ to 1 cup shrimp stock
    (see Note)

1 tablespoon tomato paste

⅓ cup heavy cream

2 teaspoons Worcestershire
    sauce

2 dashes of Tabasco sauce

Salt

2 tablespoons chopped flat-
    leaf parsley

To make the grits: Bring 3½ cups water to a boil and stir in the
grits. Reduce the heat to low, cover, and cook for 15 to 20 minutes,
until the grits are tender and the liquid has been absorbed. Remove

from the heat, add salt to taste, add the cheese and butter, and stir until melted. Keep warm.

To prepare the shrimp: Melt the butter in a large skillet over medium heat and sauté the onion, bell pepper, and garlic until softened, about 3 minutes. Add the tomatoes and juice and the thyme and bring to a simmer. Cook for 2 or 3 minutes. Sprinkle with the flour and stir well. Add the shrimp and stir constantly until they begin to turn pink, about 2 minutes. Add ½ cup stock and cook for 2 to 3 minutes more. Add the tomato paste and stir until blended. Add the cream, Worcestershire, and Tabasco, and more stock if needed to make a spoonable sauce that generously coats the shrimp. Heat thoroughly, being careful not to let it come to a boil. Taste for salt and adjust if necessary.

Place a portion of grits in the center of each plate and spoon shrimp over or around it. Sprinkle with chopped parsley.

NOTE: To make the shrimp stock: Combine the shrimp shells and 2 cups water and boil until the liquid is reduced by half. Strain.

SAUCE RÉMOULADE

YIELD: ABOUT 2 CUPS

• • •

2 large egg yolks

¼ cup vegetable oil

½ cup finely chopped
scallions

½ cup finely chopped celery

¼ cup chopped fresh
parsley leaves

¼ cup prepared horseradish

¼ lemon, seeded and cut
up (including rind)

1 bay leaf, crumbled

2 tablespoons Creole
mustard

2 tablespoons ketchup

2 tablespoons
Worcestershire sauce

1 tablespoon Dijon mustard

1 tablespoon white wine
vinegar

1 tablespoon Tabasco sauce

1 tablespoon minced garlic

3 tablespoons drained
capers

2 teaspoons sweet paprika

1 teaspoon salt

Place the yolks in a blender or food processor and blend for 2 minutes. With the machine running, add the oil gradually in a thin stream until the emulsion is thickened. One at a time, add the remaining ingredients and process until well blended and the lemon rind is finely chopped. Transfer the dressing to a covered container and chill at least 2 hours.

NOTE: This should be enough to toss with a pound and a half of medium to large shrimp.

SHRIMP TORTILLITAS

½ cup all-purpose flour

½ cup chickpea flour

1 teaspoon salt

½ pound shrimp, shelled and finely chopped

¼ cup chopped onion

2 tablespoons chopped flat-leaf parsley

Vegetable or safflower oil for frying

In a medium bowl, whisk the flours with the salt and gradually whisk in 1 cup water until smooth. Stir in the shrimp, onion, and parsley. (The batter can be prepared up to 3 hours ahead and left in a cool place.)

Pour oil to a depth of ¼ inch in a large skillet and heat over high heat until smoking. Drop the batter by tablespoonfuls into oil, spreading it with a spoon to make thin, lacy pancakes. (You will be able to cook about 4 at a time.) Fry for about 1 minute, until golden underneath, and turn to brown the other side. Drain and serve immediately.

Making the Cut

❁

I have always found it puzzling that while millions of songs have been written about love, and by extension sex, a mere handful have been written about food or eating, which is at least as important and often more satisfying. There's a great song I remember from my childhood called "Just a Bowl of Butter Beans," but it doesn't even have its own music—it's sung to the tune of "Just a Closer Walk with Thee." We are reminded that "The Lady is a Tramp" because "she gets too hungry for dinner at 8," and among the pleasures of being taken "out to the ball game" is the box of Cracker Jacks. But I think we deserve more. If there is, for example, "Shall We Dance?" why not "Shall We Dine?"

Fortunately, my friend Jimmy Phillips, who also wrote the immortal "Fried Chicken," has once again stepped up to the plate, as it were, with "Gnawing Bone." In the song (which he wrote with Billy Earl McClelland), a man returns home to find his door open and his house empty. He figures out what's going on as soon as he hits the kitchen: "The whole place smells like pork chops/But ain't no pig meat on the stove/Just some cold grease in a skillet/And one lowdown gnawing bone." It was, of course, his woman, who "even took the turnip greens." A rather more jaunty tune, "Save the Bones for Henry Jones," was written by the New Orleans jazz guitarist Danny Barker with Vernon Lee about a non-meat-eater at a banquet "most proper," where the other diners feast on everything from lox to chops: "We thought the chops were mellow/He said his chops were beat . . . We served the bones to Henry Jones/'Cause Henry don't eat no meat." (The song was also recorded by Nat King Cole and Johnny Mercer. In my favorite line, "demitasse" is rhymed with "pheasant under glass—class!")

As good as they are, both songs are primarily about the absence of meat, while to me pork chops have always evoked a sort of succulent ampleness, or at least they did before the National Pork Board decided to market their product as the "other white meat" and farmers began producing ridiculously lean hogs. The whole point of pork is the fat (that's what produces that tease of a smell in "Gnawing Bone," after all); if I want a skinless chicken breast with the taste and texture of packed sawdust, I'll buy one. Many other people feel the same way I do, which is why operations like Niman Ranch have developed a whole roster of independent farmers who raise fat and happy pigs for them out there in the heartland.

I met one of these farmers, Paul Willis, when I was traveling in Iowa with Howard Dean during the 2004 presidential primaries, and I think I might be able to date the demise of the Dean campaign to that visit. Willis, whose pigs wind up in fine restaurants across the country (including Café Boulud, where I had an excellent Niman Ranch chop recently), was trying to explain to Dean that the demand for tasty pork had gotten so great that there weren't enough farmers like him to satisfy it. Dean, who clearly wasn't listening to a word Willis was saying and had never heard of Niman Ranch, kept telling him that he needed to develop a market for his pork. Finally, after many Dean non-sequiturs in the form of tips based on the success of Vermont's organic milk producers,

Willis threw up his hands (not literally—he was very polite) and offered to show the candidate the hogs themselves. Dean actually demurred (what did he think we had all gotten up at six in the morning to come see?) until a cameraman and I browbeat him into it, and then he tried to make a joke of it by telling Willis, "This will be a good photo op—governor speaks to Washington lobbyists."

Things degenerated even further from there, but the pigs, happily chomping on corn, were adorable. But then pigs have always been pretty adorable, and pork chops have always been good. When I was growing up they were decidedly country fare, a staple of café plate lunches and rural kitchens, fried in black iron skillets or smothered with onions and brown gravy. These days I prepare them all kinds of ways, but when I cook them simply by pan-frying or grilling, I almost always brine them ahead of time. Soaking the chops for a day or two in a water bath with sugar, salt, and spices makes them much more tender and flavorful, but if you haven't planned ahead, much the same result can be achieved by rubbing them with salt and herbs and letting them sit at room temperature for a couple of hours.

In Burgundy, home of Dijon, chops are traditionally served in a sauce made with mustard, cream, and white wine, and there are very few pairings that are better. Richard Olney sautéed chops and sliced apples and then baked them all together with cream and mustard dribbled on top. I prefer the method here, but you could always fry up some apples and serve them on the side. (For a dish with roots closer to Normandy than Burgundy, make the same recipe but omit the mustard, deglaze the pan with Calvados instead of wine, and stir sliced sautéed Granny Smiths into the sauce itself.)

Louisianans love pork chops at least as much as the French and have equally wonderful ways of preparing them. Chief among them is to stuff them with even more pork and lots of red pepper. The recipe included here is from my good friend Joe Major, the former chef/owner at Joe's Dreyfuss Store in Livonia, Louisiana. Joe roasted more than thirty suckling pigs for my wedding rehearsal dinner, so I know he knows his way around a pork chop.

PORK CHOPS WITH DIJON SAUCE

YIELD: 4 SERVINGS

. . .

1 tablespoon butter

1 tablespoon vegetable oil

Four 1¼ -inch-thick
    center-cut rib or loin
    pork chops, bone in

Salt

Freshly ground black pepper

¼ cup chopped scallions or
    shallots

½ cup dry white wine

¾ cup chicken or veal
    stock

½ cup heavy cream

1 tablespoon Dijon mustard

1 tablespoon chopped flat-
    leaf parsley, optional

Melt the butter in the oil in a large deep skillet over high heat. Season the chops with salt and pepper, add them to the pan, and brown well, 2 to 3 minutes a side, reducing the heat slightly if the chops start to brown too quickly.

Remove the chops to a platter and pour off most of the fat from the pan. Add the scallions or shallots and cook over medium-high heat until softened, about 1 minute. Add the wine and bring to a boil, scraping the brown bits off the bottom of the pan. Stir in the stock and return the chops to the pan. Bring the sauce to a simmer, cover, and cook until the chops are tender, 15 to 20 minutes.

Remove the chops to a warm platter; cover with aluminum foil to keep warm. Raise the heat and boil the pan juices to reduce by half, about 2 minutes. Add the cream and boil 2 minutes more, or until the sauce reduces a bit and thickens. Remove from the heat and whisk in the mustard and chopped parsley, if using. Taste and add more mustard if desired. Immediately spoon the sauce over the chops and serve.

BRINE-CURED PORK CHOPS

. . .

FOR THE BRINE

¾ cup kosher salt

⅔ cup sugar

20 whole juniper berries

20 whole allspice berries

1 teaspoon whole black peppercorns

4 bay leaves

3 sprigs fresh thyme

3 sprigs fresh marjoram

FOR THE CHOPS

Six 1½-inch-thick center-cut rib or loin pork chops, bone in

Olive oil

Freshly ground black pepper

12 to 15 sprigs fresh rosemary, optional

Salt

To make the brine: Dissolve the salt and sugar in 1 gallon of warm water in a large bowl. In a mortar, slightly crush the juniper and allspice berries and the peppercorns along with the bay leaves and herbs; add to the brine. When the brine is cool, add the pork chops and completely submerge them, by topping with a weighted plate if necessary. Refrigerate for at least 2 days and up to 3 days.

To prepare the chops: Remove them from the brine about 2 hours before cooking and pat them dry with paper towels. Rub them with a bit of olive oil and black pepper. (You may also perfume the meat at this point with a few sprigs of fresh rosemary, placed on top of and beneath the chops.) Allow the chops to come to room temperature.

Grill the chops (partially covered if possible to control flaming) over medium-hot coals, 5 to 7 minutes a side, or fry three at a time in two preheated heavy-bottomed skillets over medium-high heat. Place them on a warm platter and cover loosely with foil. Allow them to rest about 10 minutes. Sprinkle with salt if needed.

JOE MAJOR'S STUFFED PORK CHOPS

* * *

Four 1¼ to 1½-inch-thick center-cut loin chops, bone in

1 pound finely ground pork (preferably Boston butt shoulder—the fattier the better)

4 garlic cloves, finely chopped

1 bunch scallions, thinly sliced

1 egg white

Salt

Coarsely ground black pepper

Crushed dried red chile pepper or hot red pepper flakes

½ cup all-purpose flour

¼ cup vegetable oil

1 medium yellow onion, chopped

1 green bell pepper, chopped

1 celery rib, chopped

1 cup chicken stock

Pinch of dried thyme

1 bay leaf

Insert a boning knife in the side of each chop and cut a deep pocket to within ½ inch of the bone, being careful to keep the opening only large enough to insert the tip of a pastry bag. (Or ask your butcher to do this for you.)

Put the ground pork, garlic, scallions, egg white, ¼ cup water, salt, and the black and red peppers to taste in a bowl and mix well. Pack the mixture into a pastry bag and pipe one-fourth of it into the pocket of each chop. Season the chops with salt and black pepper and dredge in flour.

Heat the oil in a heavy skillet over high heat, add the chops, and brown 2 minutes on each side. Remove them from the pan and add the onion, bell pepper, and celery. Sauté until the onions are transparent, about 3 minutes, then add the stock, scraping up any brown bits from the bottom of the pan. Return the chops to the skillet, add the thyme and bay leaf, cover, and simmer 15 minutes. Turn the chops and simmer 15 to 20 minutes more. Remove the chops and let them stand 5 minutes before serving.

Classic from a Can

❖

When I was growing up, I knew tuna salad exclusively as that excellent mixture of water-packed white tuna, mayonnaise, hard-boiled eggs, onion, celery, and sweet pickle that my mother made and that resided pretty much perpetually in our refrigerator. I ate it in the summers standing at the kitchen counter, in sloppy forkfuls straight out of the bowl. During the school year I toted it in my red plaid metal lunchbox, spread on white bread wrapped tightly in Saran Wrap and accompanied by a baggie of Lay's potato chips. I was almost thirty before I realized that tuna salad (the mayonnaise variety) existed in many other forms.

By then I'd moved to New York and gone to work at *Vogue*, where, in the pre-laptop days when I actually went to the office every day, I often ate lunch at my desk. Imagine my surprise the first time I ordered tuna salad from Mangia, the upscale carryout and café on 48th Street that served as our canteen, when it arrived flecked with shredded carrots and dill. It was delicious, and since then I have come to realize that Manhattan is a tuna salad lover's paradise. There is the rather dry version containing nothing but capers at my old neighborhood market, Butterfield, and the wet version with red onion at the stupendously wonderful Eli's. I've had the lemon-and-dill tuna salad at Whole Foods, where even a version with cranberries (they must have had a lot left over after Thanksgiving one year) is growing on me. There is the one with light mayonnaise favored by the thin and gorgeous *Vogue* assistants at the Frank Gehry-designed *Condé Nast* cafeteria (since my office days, we've moved to Times Square), and the salad of canned smoked tuna that is one of no less than three versions offered in the cafeteria of *The New York Times*.

Some versions are not so successful, however. I found a particularly revolting-sounding one in the cookbook published by the Assistance League of Omaha (inexplicably on my mother's bookshelf) containing shredded zucchini, apples, Swiss cheese, and chopped pecans. And the other day, in New Orleans, I bought a container with hidden chunks of cheddar, which is, I can now say with certainty, a disgusting idea (as opposed to melted cheddar on top of an open-faced tuna salad sandwich, which is a good idea and which makes it a tuna melt, but I'll get to that in a minute).

Proof that Southern Junior League cookbooks are superior (and that Southerners like to put gelatin in almost everything) is furnished by the very good congealed tuna salads I have recently found in at least three of them. I can especially recommend the tuna salad mold topped with cucumber mayonnaise from *Southern Sideboards* (Jackson, Mississippi). If I were the kind of person who gave ladies' luncheons, I would serve it, with homemade melba toast and maybe a fresh fruit salad on the side.

With the cheesy exceptions above, I am open to tuna salad in almost any form, but some people have extremely strong views on the subject. David Rosengarten, in *It's All American Food*, says the only tuna salad that really does it for him contains tuna, mayonnaise, and occasionally some finely chopped celery; a mixture that is then "beaten to a pulp," in the style of old-fashioned New York delis (where, he correctly points out, the tuna salad resembles "smooth tuna pate"). Also, it must be on soft supermarket white bread and, if possible, made a few hours ahead of time and wrapped in foil, "so as to simulate the conditions of the sandwich that I carried to school in my lunchbox."

I am fairly sure I won't make Rosengarten's version—he says he wants to eat it every time he returns from a foreign trip—but I understand his nostalgia. (His book, after all, is subtitled *The Foods We Really Eat, the Dishes We Will Always Love.*) He is also nostalgic about the quality of canned tuna, a product that he says he feels is on a major decline. Among the mass-produced varieties, Rosengarten insists that albacore packed in oil has by far the most flavor and the best texture and further that the oil doesn't alter the taste of the tuna salad. He says the brand closest to the canned stuff of his youth is Progresso tuna in olive oil. This will come as a big surprise to water-packed fans everywhere, including my mother. Perhaps they should try tuna packed in its own juices, a relatively new product from boutique canneries that have sprung up on the coast of Northern California and in the Pacific Northwest. Two brands Rosengarten recommends in his book are the Great American Smokehouse and Seafood Company's Deluxe Albacore Tuna from Harbor, Oregon (www.smokehouse-salmon.com; [800] 828-3474) and Dave's Homestyle Albacore Fillets from Santa Cruz, California (www.davesalbacore.com; [888] 454-8862). He finds it "too dry" to eat by itself. "But when you whip it up with a whole lotta mayo, you get the best-textured, best-tasting tuna salad ever."

Of course, you can go one better and make tuna salad from fresh tuna. This radical idea never occurred to me until I ate the amazing tuna club sandwich at the Union Square Café. This sandwich, on sourdough bread with arugula and crisp thick slices of bacon, is so incredibly good that it is now the only thing I order for lunch at the restaurant. The menu is full of many other fabulous offerings, but I can't be tempted, and no wonder.

The tuna is cooked in a court bouillon until it is well done and flaky, so as to resemble an ultra-version of the stuff from a can. It is then mixed with a sort of ultra-mayonnaise (in the form of lemon-pepper aioli), along with onion, red and yellow bell peppers, and herbs and spices. The result is not fussy and not overly "gourmet," and no single flavor overpowers the thing. Before I looked up the recipe in the restaurant's cookbook, I couldn't even isolate what made it so good. It simply tastes like the best old-fashioned tuna salad sandwich you've ever tasted, and certainly takes the "I'll-have-a-tuna-salad-on-white-for-lunch" habit to new, highly satisfying heights.

Another great tuna sandwich is Rosengarten's tuna melt on rye. He makes the salad with Hellman's, red onion, celery, and lemon juice; updates the concept by adding thin-sliced avocado between the bread and the salad; and tops the whole thing with good quality, grated, sharp cheddar before running it under the broiler. If the Union Square's sandwich is my new favorite lunch, Rosengarten's melt is my favorite soothing supper. And of course, my mother's tuna salad remains my favorite of all time.

UNION SQUARE CAFÉ'S TUNA CLUB SANDWICH

. . .

FOR THE LEMON-PEPPER AIOLI

2 egg yolks

1½ tablespoons lemon juice

2 teaspoons red wine vinegar

1 tablespoon Dijon mustard

2 teaspoons finely minced garlic

½ teaspoon kosher salt

1½ cups olive oil

¾ teaspoon coarsely ground black pepper

FOR THE POACHED TUNA

½ cup coarsely chopped onion

⅓ cup coarsely chopped carrot

⅓ cup sliced celery

1 bay leaf

3 whole black peppercorns

1 pound yellowfin tuna, skinless, cut into 2-inch pieces

FOR THE TUNA SALAD

1 teaspoon fennel seeds

2 tablespoons diced red bell pepper

2 tablespoons diced yellow bell pepper

¼ cup minced red onion

1 tablespoon julienned fresh basil leaves

1 teaspoon finely chopped mint

¾ teaspoon kosher salt

Freshly ground black pepper

Fresh lemon juice

12 slices sourdough, white, or whole wheat bread, lightly
   toasted

2½ cups arugula, trimmed, washed, and dried

Eight ¼-inch-thick slices slab bacon, cooked until crisp

To make the aioli: Combine the egg yolks, lemon juice, vinegar, mustard, garlic, and salt in a food processor. With the machine
running, slowly add the olive oil in a slow, steady stream through
the feed tube until all the oil is absorbed and the mixture has the
consistency of mayonnaise. Season to taste with black pepper and
mix for 10 seconds. Transfer to a bowl, cover, and refrigerate.

To poach the tuna: Combine 4 cups water, the onion, carrot,
celery, bay leaf, and peppercorns in a 2-quart saucepan and bring
to a boil over high heat. Lower to a simmer, cover, and cook for 15
minutes. Add the tuna pieces and simmer until they are barely
cooked through, about 10 minutes.

To make the tuna salad: Remove the cooked tuna from the
cooking liquid to a bowl using a slotted spoon. While the fish is still
warm, flake it into small pieces with a fork or your fingers. (The fish
firms up as it cools and will not flake as nicely.) Cover loosely and
let cool.

Crush the fennel seeds between two sheets of waxed paper;
then dry-fry in a small skillet until fragrant. Place in a large bowl;
add ½ cup of the aioli, the red and yellow bell peppers, red onion,
herbs, and salt and set aside.

Mix the flaked tuna into the fennel mixture. Combine well and taste for seasonings, adding salt, pepper, and lemon juice as needed. (The tuna salad can be made ahead to this point without the herbs and refrigerated until the next day; stir in the herbs just before using.)

To assemble the sandwiches: Spread a slice of sourdough bread with the aioli, then with a spoonful of the tuna salad. Top with a few leaves of the arugula and one slice of bacon. Repeat with a second slice of sourdough. Stack one layer on top of another and finish by topping with a third slice of sourdough. Repeat to make three more club sandwiches. Slice each sandwich into halves or thirds and secure each piece with a toothpick.

MY MOTHER'S TUNA SALAD

YIELD: ABOUT 3 CUPS

. . .

One 12-ounce can Star-
Kist white albacore
tuna in water
½ cup Hellmann's
mayonnaise
4 large celery ribs, peeled
and finely chopped
3 hard-boiled eggs,
chopped
3 tablespoons chopped

sweet pickles, with
their juice
1 tablespoon minced onion
1 teaspoon celery salt
1 teaspoon McCormick
Season-All
6 dashes of Tabasco sauce
Cracked pepper
Salt

Drain the tuna, place it in a bowl, and break it up with a fork. Add ¼ cup of the mayonnaise and blend well. Mix in the remaining ingredients, then add the rest of the mayonnaise. Season to taste with celery salt, Season-All, salt, and pepper. This tuna salad is better if it sits at least 1 hour before serving.

The Picnic Papers

❖

There is a great scene in Robert Lewis Taylor's biography *W.C. Fields: His Follies and Fortunes* in which Fields gets it in his head to organize a picnic for his secretary, Magda Michael; his companion, Carlotta Monti; her sister, Susie; and himself. He orders the chauffeur to "tune up the big Lincoln," the one with the silver-plated engine and built-in refrigerator, while he gets busy unlocking his liquor room, which was secured by two iron bars and four padlocks (Fields forever thought people were stealing from him). He brings out a case of Lanson 1928 champagne, six bottles of good burgundy, six bottles of sauternes, several bottles of gin, and a case of beer. He then takes the girls to the Vendome, a Los Angeles gourmet shop, where he buys caviar, pâté de foie gras, anchovies, smoked oysters, baby shrimps, crabmeat, tinned lobster, potted chicken and turkey, several cheeses, a big bottle of Greek olives, and three or four jars of glazed fruit. Back home, his cook, Dell, has made an angel food cake, a devil's food cake, and sandwiches (watercress, tongue, peanut butter and strawberry jam, chopped olives and nuts, deviled egg, and spiced ham). When the food has been packed in wicker hampers and the booze has been loaded into the fridge with many extra ice buckets, Fields ushers his passengers into the car. "What we've missed," he says, "we'll pick up on the road."

Fields was famously excessive, of course (at one point during the outing he stopped at a jewelry store and bought a half-dozen clocks for everyone in his party, including the driver), but his group did manage to get two days of sustenance out of this movable feast.

Most of us, though, lack a Dell on demand or the big Lincoln or such a generously stocked liquor cabinet, and must exercise a bit more restraint and forethought when planning a picnic.

Alice Waters thinks picnic planning should focus on the color and texture of the food, since everything is laid out all at once. It is true that a good picnic should be a tableau of sorts—think Monet's *Déjeuner sur l'Herbe* (as opposed to Manet's, where the nude, not the food, takes center stage). Pale green grapes, deep red plums, and yellowy peaches are laid out on a white cloth with a baguette, a bottle of wine, what looks like a terrine of some kind, or maybe a roast bird, and surrounded with grass in such a perfect shade of green that you want to lie down in the picture.

James Beard called picnicking "one of the supreme pleasures of outdoor life." In James Beard's *Menus for Entertaining*, he included a whole chapter on picnics, all falling somewhere between the Fields' and Waters' models. An "Elegant Picnic for the Beach" features a Roquefort cheese log covered in chopped pecans, eggs stuffed with foie gras and truffles, chicken sandwiches, foie gras sandwiches, fresh peach ice cream and, to drink, "nothing will do but iced Champagne."

Franklin Roosevelt loved picnics because they were the only meals that the dreaded White House cook, Mrs. Nesbitt, who believed in "plain foods, plainly prepared," did not make for him. Edmund Wilson seems as unlikely a picnicker as F.D.R., but for seventy years he regularly spread out a blanket on Flat Rock on the Sugar River, which ran behind his house in Talcottville in upstate

New York. It was there that the writer Frederick Exley took Mary Pcolar, Wilson's good friend and typist, just after the great man died, "a gesture to the ghost of Wilson." The scene, from Exley's novel-memoir, *Pages From a Cold Island*, begins with Exley, nervous about the meeting and "absolutely loony with industry," preparing the picnic itself: "fried" chicken breasts made with Shake 'n Bake; banana bread, sliced and spread with cream cheese to make sandwiches; a chocolate marble coconut cake from a mix, iced with Hershey's Dutch chocolate frosting. He wraps the sandwiches "individually and ever so neatly in wax paper," puts radishes and celery in a container, cuts some cheddar cheese into "delicately edible bits," and sets aside a half-dozen apples, a bunch of grapes, and four cans of black raspberry soda. Then, still afraid there's not enough to eat, he makes three of his "famous" tuna fish, egg, and onion sandwiches with the crusts trimmed off.

Exley was a mess, but the image of him preparing a picnic for this middle-aged woman who was loved by Edmund Wilson gets me every time. There is something touching about the care that goes into packing a picnic for someone else, wrapping up everything, packing the hamper, and then unpacking and unwrapping as though offering gifts.

I hit on my own picnic menu more than twenty years ago when I took supper in a hamper to a man with no functional kitchen but a very nice backyard. I only vaguely remember the man, but the menu remains my standby. At its center is the simplest recipe for roast chicken I've ever found, from the sculptor Elizabeth Frink, who contributed it to the now out-of-print *Artists' and Writers' Cookbook*. Not only is the chicken good cold, it makes the most delicious sandwiches (another picnic staple, best on thin-sliced brioche or Pepperidge Farm white with butter or a little homemade mayonnaise, salt, and black pepper) because the meat is infused with the taste of lemon. I also pack asparagus spears with a dipping sauce, a French potato salad, a crusty baguette with a spread of butter and feta cheese, and maybe some Niçoise olives. Alice Waters would probably tell me I needed some cherries or plums in there for color, or better yet, if you're still thinking painters, think Bonnard and his gorgeous *Tarte aux Cerises*.

ELIZABETH FRINK'S
ROAST LEMON CHICKEN

Adapted from The Artists' and Writers' Cookbook

YIELD: 4 SERVINGS

, , ,

2 lemons

One 3-pound chicken

½ teaspoon salt

¼ teaspoon freshly ground black pepper

6 cloves garlic, peeled

2 tablespoons butter

2 tablespoons olive oil

1 tablespoon coarsely chopped flat-leaf parsley

Preheat the oven to 325 degrees. Cut one lemon into eight pieces. Place the chicken in a large baking dish and rub the peel side of the lemon pieces over the outside of the chicken. Season inside and out with salt and pepper. Put the 8 lemon pieces inside the chicken along with the garlic cloves. In a small pan, melt the butter with the olive oil and pour on top and inside the chicken.

Roast the chicken for 1½ hours, until an instant-read thermometer inserted in the thickest part of the leg registers 180 degrees. Half an hour before the chicken is done, pour the juice from the second lemon over the chicken and sprinkle with chopped parsley.

ASPARAGUS WITH SAUCE ALSACIENNE

YIELD: 4 SERVINGS

* * *

1 pound asparagus

2 large eggs

1 tablespoon Dijon mustard

½ teaspoon salt

1 tablespoon red wine vinegar

1 cup vegetable oil

1½ tablespoons finely chopped shallots

3 tablespoons finely chopped flat-leaf parsley

1 tablespoon finely chopped fresh basil or tarragon

Trim the ends off the asparagus and place them in a pot of boiling salted water. Bring the water to a second boil, reduce the heat, and boil slowly, uncovered, for 2 to 5 minutes, until the spears bend a little but are not limp. Drain and rinse them under cold running water until cool. Spread the cooked spears in a single layer on paper towels so they will finish cooling quickly.

Place the eggs on a spoon and lower into a small saucepan of boiling water. Boil the eggs for 3 minutes (3½ if they are chilled). Rinse under cold running water until cool enough to handle. Hit each egg with a knife at "the equator" and pull the halves apart. With a spoon, pull out the yolks into a medium-size bowl. Set aside the whites, in their shells, to finish cooking.

Whisk the yolks until they are thick and sticky. Whisk in the mustard, salt, and vinegar. Add the oil, whisking by hand or with an electric mixer, drop by drop at first and then in a slow, steady stream. When all the oil is incorporated, stir in the shallots, parsley, and basil or tarragon and taste for salt. Sieve or finely chop the egg whites and fold them in, if desired. If the sauce is too thick for dipping, thin with a little vinegar.

FRENCH POTATO SALAD

YIELD: 4 SERVINGS

* * *

2 pounds small russet potatoes

¼ cup dry white wine

1 tablespoon white wine vinegar

1 tablespoon fresh lemon juice

1 teaspoon Dijon mustard

½ teaspoon salt

¼ teaspoon white pepper

¼ cup olive oil

2 tablespoons finely chopped scallions

2 tablespoons finely chopped flat-leaf parsley

Scrub the potatoes and drop them into a saucepan of enough boiling salted water to cover. Boil for about 30 minutes, or just until the potatoes are tender when pierced with a small knife. Drain. As soon as the potatoes are cool enough to handle, peel and cut them into ⅛-inch-thick slices. Place the potatoes in a large shallow serving dish. Pour the wine over the warm slices and toss very gently. Set aside until the potatoes have absorbed the wine.

Meanwhile, use a small whisk to beat the vinegar, lemon juice, mustard, salt, and white pepper in a small bowl until the salt has dissolved. Add the oil by droplets, and whisk until thickened. Whisk in the scallion. Pour the dressing over the potatoes and toss gently. Recheck seasoning and adjust if necessary. Sprinkle with the chopped parsley.

CHERRY TART

* * *

FOR THE TART SHELL

1 cup all-purpose flour

1 tablespoon sugar

¼ teaspoon salt

¼ teaspoon grated lemon zest

8 tablespoons (1 stick) unsalted butter

1 tablespoon water

½ teaspoon vanilla extract

FOR THE CHERRY FILLING

9 tablespoons sugar

1 cup red Bordeaux wine

2 tablespoons fresh lemon juice

3 cups fresh Bing cherries, rinsed, stemmed, and pitted

FOR THE ALMOND CUSTARD

1 large egg

1 egg yolk

¾ cup sugar

½ cup all-purpose flour

1 cup whole milk

3 tablespoons butter

2 tablespoons cognac or kirsch

2 teaspoons vanilla extract

¼ teaspoon almond extract

½ cup whole blanched almonds, finely ground in a food
    processor or blender

To make the tart shell: Mix the flour, sugar, salt, and lemon zest in a bowl or food processor. Cut the butter into ½-inch slices and work them into the flour mixture with your fingers, or use the pulse motion of your processor, until the mixture is mostly cornmeal-size pieces and begins to hold together. Combine the water and vanilla and work them into the mixture just until the pastry is well blended and will hold together if you press it. Press the dough evenly over the bottom and up the sides of a 9-inch tart pan. Wrap the tart pan in foil and freeze for 30 minutes, or overnight.

Preheat the oven to 375 degrees. Lightly press in a sheet of aluminum foil to line the bottom and sides of the tart shell and fill with pie weights or dried beans. Bake the shell for about 25 minutes, or until the edges are golden brown. Carefully lift off the weights and foil. Bake the shell 5 minutes more. Cool the tart shell in the pan on a wire rack.

While the tart shell bakes, make the cherry filling: Combine 6 tablespoons of the sugar, the wine, and the lemon juice in a medium saucepan and stir until the sugar is dissolved. Heat to boiling. Drop in the cherries and simmer for 5 minutes, or until they are just tender. Cool the cherries in the syrup for 30 minutes; then drain, saving the syrup for another use. (It can be kept covered in the refrigerator for up to 2 weeks.)

Meanwhile, make the almond crust: Whisk the egg and egg yolk in a mixing bowl until blended and gradually whisk in the sugar until the mixture is pale yellow. Whisk in the flour. Heat the milk to boiling in a small saucepan and whisk it into the egg mixture in a thin stream, continuing to whisk until smooth. Pour the mixture into a medium saucepan and cook over medium heat, whisking slowly, until the mixture coagulates into lumps. Whisk vigorously until the custard is smooth. Lower the heat and beat with a wooden spoon 2 to 3 minutes more to cook the flour thoroughly. Remove the saucepan from the heat; beat in the butter, cognac, and extracts. Fold in the almonds and the drained cherries.

Preheat the broiler. Spread the filling in the tart shell. Sprinkle the remaining 3 tablespoons of sugar over the tart and broil 2 to 3 minutes to caramelize the sugar lightly.

Rich and Famous

❖

In *Lady Baltimore*, Owen Wister's ornate 1906 novel of American manners set in the post–Civil War South, the protagonist, John Mayrant, is engaged to a "steel wasp" of dubious background. (She is from either Natchez or Mobile; her father, a Confederate general, is said to have fled the Battle of Chattanooga.) She smokes, drinks highballs, and consorts with other men, including a New York banker she uses to investigate the magnitude of her future husband's fortune. However, in the eyes of the narrator, the gravest of her sins is that she pretends to be so financially strapped that the prospective groom must arrange the details of the wedding himself. This includes ordering the cake—a Lady Baltimore—from the Woman's Exchange tearoom.

Though the cake business takes place as the novel opens, John has already realized he may have made a mistake. But he is a man of honor, and this is turn-of-the-century Charleston (Wister changed the city's name to Kings Port on the advice of his friend Henry James), where honor is pretty much all there is left. Finally, after a lot of tortured goings-on and some not very well disguised lectures from the author on North-South relations and the wisdom of the Fifteenth Amendment, our hero finds a way to release himself from his previous engagement and marry the girl he really loves. It was the Lady Baltimore cake that did it—the bride turns out to be the sweet plantation girl he ordered it from.

It is no wonder that this cake plays such a key role in the novel. It is really, really good, a fact the narrator, a Yankee who eats a piece for lunch almost every day, comments on with frequency. ("Oh, my goodness! Did you ever taste it? It's all soft, and it's in layers, and it has nuts—but I can't write any more about it; my mouth waters too much.") It turns out that there really was a Woman's Exchange in Charleston, and legend has it that Owen Wister was served a piece of the cake there by its creator, Alicia Rhett Mayberry. But in the years since, its popularity has grown far beyond that city. A light, three-layer "silver" cake (meaning that it is made with egg whites instead of yolks), it has a filling containing dried figs, pecans, raisins, and a bit of brandy or sherry. It is indeed grand enough for a wedding, and its fame spawned a Lord Baltimore cake (made with yolks instead of whites, and whose filling contains macaroon crumbs, toasted almonds, and candied cherries).

No one can tell me why Mrs. Mayberry, a native of Charleston, named the cake Lady Baltimore, but there was such a woman. Her name was Joan Calvert, second wife of George Calvert, the first Lord Baltimore, who founded the first religiously tolerant colony in North America (Avalon, a refuge for Catholics fleeing English penal laws, on the southern coast of Newfoundland) whose heirs founded St. Mary's City, the first settlement in what is now Maryland. Mrs. Calvert, a rather homely woman with jet-black ringlets, seems unlikely to have inspired such a rapturous cake. It's more likely there was a fad for using her title, which has been given to everything from a silver pattern to a species of African violet. And while her cake is probably the most famous one named after someone, there are plenty more.

Usually cakes are named for famous people who like them. There's a Robert E. Lee cake, a popular (during his lifetime) sponge cake with a citrusy filling the general is said to have loved, and a Robert Redford cake that the legendary baker Maida Heatter read about in *Chocolate News* magazine. (Redford was reported to have been wild about a chocolate cake sweetened with honey he ate in a Manhattan restaurant, so Heatter procured the recipe and gave it his name.) There's a flourless chocolate cake named after the late Queen Mother. (It was served to her once at tea in a private house, and, the story goes, she began featuring it at royal parties.) There is even a cake, a genoise layered with kirsch-flavored *crème mousseline* and strawberries, named after an American bandleader, Ray Ventura, who was popular in France just after World War II.

A carrot cake is often called a Queen Anne's cake in England, but it is named after Queen Anne's lace, the flower, which is in fact a wild carrot. In France, there are Proust's famous madeleines and the cupcakes called *marguerites*. In this country, cakes are mass-produced and have the decidedly more downmarket names of Little Debbie and Suzy Q. A whole company named after Dolley Madison makes a dreadful chocolate cream-filled cupcake—though the real Dolley was far more famous for introducing ice cream to the White House (introduced to her by Thomas Jefferson, who had enjoyed it in Paris) at her raucous Wednesday-night receptions. I'm sure there were plenty of cakes offered on those occasions, but they wouldn't have been anything like the too-sweet chocolate sponge cake that bears her name. In those pre-baking-powder days, cakes were dense affairs, loaded with alcohol, dried fruit, and nuts.

In the mid- to late-nineteenth century, baking powder finally became reliable, so cooks deconstructed those Old English-style cakes, incorporating their booze and fruits and nuts into fillings that they then put between layers of the newly possible light and airy cakes. The Lady Baltimore and Robert E. Lee cakes are typical of Southern cakes invented in that period, as is Mrs. Emma Rylander Lane's Prize Cake. Originally published in 1898 in *Some Good Things to Eat*, the recipe for Lane Cake, as it is now known, called for a rich white cake filled with an even richer custard containing "one wine-glass full of good whiskey or brandy" and raisins. It is still popular in the South, but I've seen recipes for it everywhere, including *James Beard's Menus for Entertaining*. He adds coconut, pecans, and cherries to the filling and inexplicably refers to poor departed Mrs. Lane as Glenna McGinnis Lane.

The Mrs. Lane of my day is almost certainly Mrs. Margaret Harling, the mother of my friend the screenwriter Robert Harling and the maker of a coconut cake that is one of the best things I have ever eaten. Owen Wister would surely move to her hometown of Natchitoches, Louisiana, and come up with a novel to set there were he alive to taste it. I have always longed to be the first person to publish its recipe, which I would name, of course, Mrs. Margaret Harling's Prize Cake. Alas, though she makes it almost weekly for church bazaars and birthdays, the recipe is locked in her head and fails to work as soon as she puts it on paper. There is a long history of this problem among instinctive cooks, but I intend to persevere. Until then, I'll make do with generous gifts from Mrs. Harling and, of course, the luscious Lady Baltimore.

LADY BALTIMORE CAKE

YIELD: 12 TO 16 SERVINGS

. . .

FOR THE CAKE LAYERS

1 cup butter, at room temperature, plus additional for
    greasing pan

2 cups sifted sugar

3½ cups cake flour

4 teaspoons baking powder

¼ teaspoon salt

1 cup milk

2 teaspoons vanilla extract

½ teaspoon almond extract

8 large egg whites, at room temperature

FOR THE FROSTING

2 cups sugar

4 large egg whites, at room temperature

Pinch of salt

1 cup walnuts or pecans, finely chopped

½ cup raisins, finely chopped

6 dried figs, coarsely chopped

1 teaspoon vanilla extract

1 teaspoon brandy or sherry, optional

Preheat the oven to 350 degrees. Grease three 8 × 2-inch round
cake pans with butter. Line the bottoms with parchment paper.
Grease the parchment paper.

To make the cake: Beat the butter and sugar in a bowl at high speed until fluffy. Sift the flour, baking powder, and salt into a bowl. Mix the milk and extracts in a measuring cup. Add the flour mixture into the butter mixture a little at a time, alternating with the milk and beating after each addition.

In a bowl, beat the egg whites at high speed until stiff. Fold into the butter mixture. Divide the batter among the pans. Bake for 25 to 30 minutes, or until golden and the cakes pull away slightly from the pan sides. Cool the cakes in the pans on wire racks for 10 minutes before turning out.

To make the frosting: Combine the sugar and ½ cup water in a saucepan, bring to a boil, and cook for 5 minutes. Meanwhile, beat the egg whites with the salt in a bowl until frothy. Continue to beat and add the hot sugar syrup in a thin stream. Keep beating at high speed until the frosting forms stiff peaks.

Mix in the nuts, raisins, figs, vanilla, and liqueur if using and stir.

Spread the frosting between the layers on top and on the sides.

ROBERT REDFORD CAKE

Adapted from Maida Heatter

YIELD: 16 SERVINGS

· · ·

FOR THE CAKE

1½ sticks unsalted butter, plus additional for greasing pan

Fine bread crumbs or flour for dusting

1 cup blanched hazelnuts or almonds

12 ounces semisweet chocolate

½ cup honey

10 eggs, separated

¼ teaspoon salt

FOR THE FROSTING

¾ cup heavy cream

12 ounces semisweet chocolate

Preheat the oven to 375 degrees. Butter a 10 by 3-inch round or springform cake pan. Line the bottom with parchment paper. Butter the parchment paper and dust with fine bread crumbs or flour. Shake out the excess.

To make the cake: Grind the nuts to a powder in a food processor. Set aside.

Break up the chocolate and melt it in the top of a double boiler over shallow, warm water on moderate heat. Transfer to a bowl and let cool.

Meanwhile, in the bowl of an electric mixer, beat the butter until soft. Gradually add the honey; beat until smooth. Add the egg yolks two or three at a time, beating until incorporated after each addition. (The mixture will look curdled, but it is okay.) Add the nuts.

In another bowl, beat the egg whites with the salt until the whites barely stand up when the beater is raised. Fold the beaten egg whites into the cooled chocolate in three batches. Pour the batter into the pan. Bake the cake at 375 degrees for 20 minutes. Reduce the temperature to 350 degrees, and bake for 50 minutes more, or until a cake tester comes out clean. Remove the cake from the oven and let it cool. Remove from the pan. With a long sharp knife, level the top.

To make the frosting: Break up the chocolate. In a saucepan over medium heat, cook the cream until it forms a skin on top. Add the chocolate, reduce the heat to low, and stir with a whisk until smooth. Transfer to a bowl and stir occasionally until cool and slightly thick. Pour the icing over the cake and smooth the top and sides until covered. Serve immediately, or store overnight at room temperature.

Frozen Assets

❖

One of my most vivid food memories is of the peach ice cream my mother made in an old-fashioned freezer (it was electric but it required ice and rock salt) one summer when I was either ten or eleven years old. It is a memory made more vivid by the fact that we never had it again, a sad truth I'm sure my mother will dispute. Making homemade ice cream for your family and friends is a wholesome, thoughtful, all-American thing to do, she will reason, the kind of thing she actually did do for us often. So surely, she will insist, she must have made it more than once. She did not. We returned to scooping up Borden's out of its rectangular carton, and greeted the opening of the first Baskin-Robbins in our town with excitement bordering on the ridiculous. Homemade ice cream became, for me, a rarefied delicacy; it was certainly not something people actually made or ate all the time.

All these years later, I have discovered that it is really, really easy to make ice cream. (Any idiot can pour cream and sugar and one or two other taste treats into a mechanized bowl and turn it on, even if you have to pack it with ice and salt.) I've also discovered that at least as much as a soufflé, ice cream is guaranteed to wow the crowds. For one thing, everybody has the same distant, glorified memory of eating it. In the very fine *American Heritage Cookbook* and *Illustrated History of Eating and Drinking* (1964), Paul Engle writes: "In summer, when ice cream (and it really had cream, not thin milk) would be made at home, there was always the dividing up of the labor between the kids, each doing a fixed number of turns on the crank. And afterward, there was the sharing of the ice cream left clinging to the dasher. Nothing in a dish, eaten with a spoon, was as full of flavor as that remnant, hardly five minutes old."

Now it is not possible to read that without wanting to immediately go out and buy an ice-cream maker with a dasher, preferably a cast-iron dasher that gets freezing cold like the one the people at the White Mountain company have put in theirs for the last 150 years. I got a White Mountain with a nice pine bucket and an electric motor from Williams-Sonoma (I am nostalgic, but not enough to want to hand crank my ice cream, which is just weird, given the options), and I highly recommend it. I also recommend the Italian models like DeLonghi and Musso that come with built-in freezers and don't require rock salt and ice. They are expensive, but do not be tempted to buy the wimpy $50 models—you have to freeze the bowl forever, and anyway, the Italians have been making ice cream a long time.

Like just about everything else in the world, ice cream supposedly originated (as "water ice") in China. Marco Polo (or somebody) toted it back to the West sometime in the thirteenth century, and ice cream as we know it—an iced, flavored dessert made from milk or cream—is thought to have been made in Italy about three hundred years later. Not long afterward, cooks in France began making the stuff, and it made its way throughout Europe and over to America. George Washington was known to have his own "Cream Machine for making Ice" at Mount Vernon and, according to *Great Desserts of the South*, spent almost $200 on the ingredients for it in the summer of 1790. Thomas Jefferson served his recipe for ice cream ("2 bottles of good cream, 6 yolks of eggs, 1⁄2 pound of sugar") in hot pastry shells, a fact that guests found highly impressive. In February 1802, a minister, Manasseh Cutler, dined on the delicacy at the White House (after a dinner that also included roast beef, mutton, turkey, ham, and veal, and "a pie called macaroni") and pronounced it "very good, crust wholly dried . . . a dish somewhat like pudding—inside white as milk or curd, very porous and light, covered with cream sauce—very fine."

The high point of James Madison's second inaugural ball in 1812 was ice cream made with cream from the president's dairy at Montpelier and topped with strawberries from the first lady's garden. At that point ice cream was already on the menu of the New Orleans Coffee Exchange, and in 1846, a hand-cranked freezer was invented (before that the ingredients were beaten by hand and shaken up and down in a pot of ice and salt).

Jefferson's recipe was for a custard-based ice cream. While the third president set a culinary standard in the White House that few inhabitants since have come close to matching, and while his taste in almost all things is not just superior but perfect, I have to say I like the straight cream-based concoctions better. Especially when the ice cream has fruit in it. A custard (made on top of the stove with egg yolks, sugar, and milk or cream) is too rich to allow the perfection of mid-summer fruit to shine through properly.

"For ice cream, genuine cream is of course preferable," wrote Annabella Hill in her 1867 cookbook. I agree, and so does one of my heroes, the Southern food historian and cookbook writer Damon Lee Fowler who, in his *Classical Southern Cooking*, praises it "for flavor, for feel on the tongue, for its pure, silken richness." It's true that ice creams made with nothing but heavy cream, sugar, and flavorings (which are sometimes referred to as "Philadelphia style") are the only ones that have that highly agreeable, slightly rough quality on the tongue. Custard ice creams are much smoother and fancier.

Having said that, there are not a whole lot of things better than the caramel (custard) ice cream I include here, adapted from one that Patrick O'Connell serves at his fabulous Inn at Little Washington, in Washington, Virginia. It is excellent as is, with a bit of rum or bourbon added, alongside a bitter chocolate soufflé or tart and, for maniacal caramel lovers, with caramel sauce. (Especially delicious is a caramel sauce heated and mixed with a bit of grated orange rind and Cointreau.) O'Connell serves a lot of ice creams, including, at times, roasted banana to go with a molten chocolate cake, and ginger, made with grated fresh and chopped candied ginger. Recipes for these are in his *The Inn at Little Washington Cookbook*, which is a good thing because I don't think most fine restaurants serve enough ice cream these days.

I grew up in an era when a crème de menthe parfait or even a good scoop of chocolate was considered de riguer on certain kinds of menus. At the late and much-lamented Justine's in Memphis, two signature, non-custard ice creams were on the menu: Garden Mint, flavored with fresh mint, fresh crushed pineapple, and a dash of crème de menthe; and the delicate Lotus, flavored with lemon juice and zest, almond extract, and chopped toasted almonds. Both were extraordinarily delicious, a fact that lets my mother off the hook since she's the one who most often took me there.

JUSTINE'S LOTUS ICE CREAM

YIELD: ABOUT 1 QUART, 4 TO 6 SERVINGS

. . .

2⅔ cups heavy cream

1 cup sugar

½ cup fresh lemon juice

⅓ cup finely chopped toasted almonds

2½ teaspoons lemon zest

½ teaspoon vanilla extract

¼ teaspoon almond extract

Combine all the ingredients in a mixing bowl and stir until the sugar is dissolved.

Pour into an ice-cream machine and process according to the manufacturer's directions.

PEACH ICE CREAM

· · ·

4 pounds ripe peaches

1¼ cups sugar (or more, as needed)

⅛ teaspoon salt

2 teaspoons lemon juice

1 quart (4 cups) heavy cream

One 2-inch piece of vanilla bean, or 2 teaspoons vanilla
   extract

Peel the peaches over a large bowl to catch the juice. Halve
and pit them and chop roughly. Place them in the bowl with the
juice and sprinkle with ½ cup of sugar, the salt, and the lemon
juice and let them sit for 30 minutes.

While the peaches macerate, put the cream and the remaining
sugar in a saucepan with the vanilla bean or extract. Heat over
medium-low heat, stirring frequently to prevent scorching, until
the sugar is dissolved. Remove from the heat and cool. Discard the
vanilla bean.

Pour the cream over the peaches and mix thoroughly. Taste to
see if it needs more sugar. (This will depend on the peaches.) Refrigerate until chilled.

Pour the mixture into an ice-cream machine and freeze according to the manufacturer's directions until set but not quite hard. (If
serving immediately, freeze harder.) Pack the ice cream into a bowl
or mold to completely solidify. When it has hardened, dip the
mold into hot water or wrap it in a hot towel and invert onto a
serving platter. Or, simply scoop and serve.

NOTE: This recipe is also delicious made with fresh mangoes.

CARAMEL ICE CREAM

YIELD: ABOUT 1½ QUARTS, 6 TO 8 SERVINGS

* * *

FOR THE CARAMEL

1¼ cups heavy cream

1½ cups sugar

½ cup (1 stick) butter

FOR THE ICE CREAM BASE

2 cups heavy cream

1 cup milk

6 egg yolks

¾ cup sugar

To make the caramel: In a heavy-bottomed saucepan, scald the cream and keep it warm. In another saucepan combine the sugar with ½ cup of water over medium heat and stir until the sugar dissolves and the liquid is clear. Turn the heat to high and boil the mixture, without stirring, until it is a light to medium amber color, about 10 minutes. Remove from the heat and slowly stir in the cream. (Protect your face and hands, because the cream will splatter.) Stir until smooth, whisk in the butter, and let cool.

To make the ice cream base: In a heavy-bottomed saucepan, scald the cream and milk. In the top of a double boiler set over simmering water, whisk the egg yolks and sugar. Add the scalded cream mixture, turn up the heat until the water in the bottom of the double boiler is boiling, and whisk the mixture continuously until it is thick enough to coat the back of a spoon. Remove the pan from the heat and whisk in the caramel.

Chill the base overnight and freeze in an ice-cream maker according to the manufacturer's directions.

144 ● Ham Biscuits, Hostess Gowns, and Other Southern Specialties

Giving a Fig

M y friend George Peterkin, Jr. is fig obsessed. He lives in
Houston and travels all the time, but from mid-June until mid-July when the figs are ripe on his trees, he refuses
to leave them. He can't. For one thing, somebody has to shoot the
squirrels when they get after them. (The birds are less of a problem.
A pair of territorial mockingbirds keep the other birds away, and
George estimates that they can only eat "maximum five percent" of
the crop by themselves. "I love those mockingbirds," he says.)
Also, the more than fifty people on his fig list would be extremely
upset.

George has fourteen fig trees—thirteen Celeste and one L.S.U.
Purple, a new variety, developed by Louisiana State University
Agricultural Center, that George does not recommend. ("They
have no taste.") These trees put out a lot of figs; he spends as much
as two or three hours a day picking them, collecting the good ones
in baskets, and tossing the ones that have "bloomed out" (the fig's
fruit is also its flower) into his neighbor's yard. The bulk of them
are then divided into brown paper bags that are picked up by or delivered to the lucky folks on the list, a diverse group that includes
former Republican secretary of state and treasury secretary James
Baker, and, until he died, the former Democratic senator, candidate for president, and treasury secretary Lloyd Bentsen.

George proudly says he is a "third generation fig man." His figs are so important to him that when he married his wife, Nancy, she had to agree to two things: she would never check a suitcase when they traveled, and she would always peel his breakfast figs. ("I've been peeling them for thirty-eight years," she confirms, with something slightly less than a smile.) I have to agree with George that the breakfast figs, served with sugar and heavy cream, are superior when they are peeled, but I'll eat them pretty much any way I can. And when visiting Nancy and George during the season, there is ample opportunity. The last time I went for a weekend of heavy fig tasting, we had figs wrapped in prosciutto; we had fig preserves on toast; we even had fig daiquiris. The flavor of the figs in the daiquiris was a bit overwhelmed by the lime juice and the rum, but the color, a pale pink, was gorgeous, and George pronounced them "just the thing for a first drink."

George's devotion to figs is touching, but he is not alone. When the legendary newspaper editor Hodding Carter, Jr. died, his son Philip wrote a tribute to him that included a list of the things he loved. Among them were "good whiskey, fresh figs, raw oysters." The Greek poet Alexis of Thurii referred to the fig as "that god-given inheritance of our mother country," and the "darling of my heart." According to *The Horizon Cookbook and Illustrated History of Eating and Drinking through the Ages*, the ancients attributed "magical, medicinal powers" to the fig; Athenaeus called it "the most useful of all the fruits which grow on trees." The Egyptians buried whole baskets of them with their dead. They valued them for their taste, of course, but also their mild laxative qualities— they believed that most illnesses had their source in the alimentary canal and were forever fasting and generally cleaning out their digestive systems.

In ancient Greece, a farmer would have grown some fig and olive trees, along with some wheat or barley, and raised pigs for meat. This remains an excellent combination. What could be better than a plate of ripe figs, good olives, slices of Italian prosciutto or Spanish Serrano ham, and a loaf of chewy bread? (When we had this same combo at George and Nancy's, the olives were in our martinis.) James Beard served figs alongside crisp bacon, and in Eric Ripert's cookbook, *A Return to Cooking*, there's a recipe for figs wrapped in bacon, baked, and accompanied by a shallot confit. Inspired by two different Jeremiah Tower recipes, I made a relish out of the figs I toted home from George's trees and served it with some thick, pan-fried pork chops. (It would also be excellent with grilled duck breast, especially a *magret* from www.dartagnan.com, chicken, or even fish.)

My mother and George have argued for years over who makes the best fig preserves. She puts lemon peel in hers; George, the purist, does not. I avoid the fight all together and happily accept jars from each. On our honeymoon, my husband and I discovered another source for them, the Carolina Cider Company in Gardens Corner, South Carolina (843-846-1899), a wonderful shack of a place that sells everything from delicious cherry cider to even more delicious pickled garlic. We also bought some fig syrup, which has been around almost as long as figs—until the end of the Middle Ages, it was often substituted for honey as a sweetener. The label says it's "great on pancakes or ice cream," and I'm sure it is, but the other night I used it along with some chopped fresh mint to marinate lamb chops.

Until I was grown, I had never tasted a fig other than a Celeste, although I didn't know what it's actual name was—most Southerners simply call it the "sugar fig." Celestes are the variety most common to the eastern United States. They are said to grow best in the Southeast, but, obviously, they also do all right in Texas. Figs don't travel well, and Celestes are extremely fragile, but these days I can get Black Mission figs from California in the grocery store, and sometimes Kadotas as well. They are shipped slightly under ripe so that they don't turn to mush, and since they are larger than Celestes, they hold up better in a lot of recipes. At Restaurant August in New Orleans, I once had a mission fig stuffed with foie gras and served on toast with a dusting of truffles and a little fig reduction. If the fig had been a sweet little Celeste, that particular preparation would have been gilding the lily, not to mention almost impossible because of its size, but this was really, really good. The restaurant's brilliant chef, John Besh, is another fig man. He gave me a terrific second course of rabbit confit with baked figs, which prompted me to do the same with some store-bought confit of duck legs at home (D'Artagnan has that, too). Fry them in a bit of the fat that will be clinging to the legs until they are crisp (four or five minutes on each side). While they cook, drizzle some halved figs with a bit of balsamic vinegar, sprinkle with fresh thyme leaves, and bake at 400 degrees for about thirty minutes (or less if the figs are Celestes).

If you are as dedicated a fig man (or woman) as George, I suggest more figs for dessert—alone or with a creamy goat cheese. Or, try Patricia Wells's fabulous fig tart, which combines them with their Mediterranean siblings, almonds and honey. I guarantee that afterward, you will try hard to find a way to get on somebody's fig list.

FIG AND ALMOND TART

Adapted from Patricia Wells At Home In Provence

YIELD: 8 SERVINGS

* * *

FOR THE TART SHELL

Softened butter for greasing the pan

8 tablespoons (1 stick) unsalted butter, melted and cooled

½ cup granulated sugar

⅛ teaspoon almond extract

⅛ teaspoon vanilla extract

Pinch of salt

1¼ cups, plus 1 tablespoon, unbleached, all-purpose flour

2 tablespoons ground, unblanched almonds

FOR THE FILLING

½ cup heavy cream

1 large egg, lightly beaten

½ teaspoon almond extract

½ teaspoon vanilla extract

2 tablespoons raw, full-flavored honey (like lavender)

1 tablespoon superfine flour (like Wondra)

1½ pounds fresh figs, halved lengthwise (don't peel)

Confectioners' sugar

Preheat the oven to 375 degrees. Butter the sides and bottom of a 9-inch tart pan with a removable bottom, or a springform pan, and set aside.

To make the tart shell: Combine the melted butter and sugar in a large bowl and blend with a wooden spoon. Add the extracts, salt, and flour and stir to form a soft, cookie-like dough. (Do not let it form into a ball.) Transfer the dough to the center of the tart pan. Using your fingers, press the dough evenly onto the bottom and sides. (It will be quite thin.) If using a springform pan, press the dough 1½ inches up the sides. Bake until the dough is slightly puffy and set, 12 to 15 minutes. Remove from the oven and sprinkle the ground almonds on the crust.

To make the filling: In a medium bowl, combine the cream, egg, extracts, and honey and whisk to blend. Whisk in the flour. Starting just inside the edge of the tart shell, neatly overlap the figs, cut side up, at a slight angle. Make two or three concentric circles, working toward the center, and fill the center with the remaining figs.

Rewhisk the cream mixture and pour evenly over the fruit. Place the tart in the center of the oven with a baking sheet on the rack below to catch any drips. Bake until the filling is firm and the pastry a deep golden brown, 50 to 60 minutes. Remove and sprinkle with confectioners' sugar just before serving.

NOTE: Unpeeled apricots or plums may be substituted for figs.

FIG RELISH

Adapted from Jeremiah Tower's New American Classics

YIELD: ABOUT 2 CUPS

· · ·

1 medium red onion, finely chopped (about ½ cup)

8 large fresh ripe Mission figs, finely chopped (or about 20
    Celestes)

1 to 2 fresh serrano chiles, stemmed, seeded, and finely
    chopped

½ cup fresh mint leaves

¼ cup fresh lime juice

1 teaspoon salt

1 teaspoon freshly ground black pepper

Soak the chopped onion in ice water for 10 minute; rinse, and pat dry with paper towels. Combine the onion and figs and half the chiles in a bowl.

Blanch the mint leaves in boiling water for 1 minute and cool immediately in ice water. Drain, squeeze dry, and finely chop. Add to the fig mixture. Add the lime juice, salt, and black pepper. Stir well and taste and adjust seasoning if needed. Add as much of the remaining chili as desired. Let sit for 1 hour so the flavors can develop.

JUDY REED'S FIG PRESERVES

, , ,

4 cups figs

1 cup sugar

½ lemon, thinly sliced and seeded

Trim the stem ends and rinse the figs. Put the figs into a heavy-bottomed saucepan with the sugar, lemon slices, and 1 cup water. Simmer over low heat, stirring occasionally, until a thick syrup forms.

Transfer the hot figs to two sterilized 1-pint Mason-type jars, top with sterilized lids, and seal in a hot-water bath according to the jar manufacturer's directions. Cool and store in a dark place.

Extremely Gifted

❖

During the holidays, I tend to err on the side of extravagance. One year I held so many back-to-back gatherings that my friend Elizabeth gave me a guest towel reading, "A fool and his money can throw a hell of a party." She sure can. When one seated dinner expanded to include more people than I had plates, I simply bought some more—lovely old green glass ones from the divine Niall Smith in Manhattan. Even he urged me to think about them overnight, but I didn't want to. They were so beautiful and so festive I just had to have them.

The women in my family have always gone a little crazy at Christmas. When all my friends were getting things like baby dolls and tricycles as presents, my grandmother presented my spoiled self with a merry-go-round (a real one, one that you could ride) and a car (a motorized Stutz Bearcat that I drove all around our yard). About twenty years ago, my mother, a woman who puts more than seventy strings of white lights on her Christmas tree each year and who once insisted on hanging a stocking for our pet goldfish, decided to make an attempt at frugality and put up pickles to give as presents. But she never actually cut back on the gifts she bought, and now the pickle list has grown to sixty. She has also been known to give a few parties herself, although my father finally shut down our "neighborhood" Christmas night party after it grew to include half the people in town and all their visiting relations.

Recently, however, I've decided to buck the gene pool and adjust my spending to the Dow Jones. I am still going to shop, of course, but I intend to clock at least as much time in the grocery store as on Madison Avenue. And instead of prepping for parties, I am going to make presents.

The first time I made this vow I was twelve and did not yet earn my own living. I took a tip from *Glamour* (a magazine that also advised me to spray-paint an old pair of shoes silver for a sparkly holiday effect) and made my piano teacher, our next-door neighbors, and my grandparents gifts of brandied peaches, said to be a perfect accompaniment to pound cake or vanilla ice cream. Looking back on it, I realize that the peaches were about as successful as the shoes. And just as gross and sticky, consisting as they did of canned peach halves studded with cloves, a handful of bottled maraschino cherries, a shot of brandy, and a cinnamon stick. My second foray into homemade gifts, jars of hot fudge sauce, was even less of a triumph. The sauce itself, from *The Silver Palate Cookbook*, was delicious. The problem arose from the fact that since I had waited until Christmas Eve to make it, I was in a hurry and did not exactly allow the sauce a whole lot of time to cool before putting it into the jars. Had the holiday weather in the Mississippi Delta been its usual 40 or 50 degrees, things still would have turned out all right. But that particular year was the only time I can remember when the temperature dropped below 10. I had barely made it out of our driveway when the first jar exploded all over the backseat of my father's brand-new Buick.

That was more than twenty-five years ago, and I haven't tried much since. I'm happy to say, though, that I have been on the receiving end of some very tasty loot. Especially from the kitchen of my friend Mary Youngblood Cooper. Mary can do anything: She canes chairs, she's an excellent gardener, she even makes her own cheese. And at Christmas she always makes me the best pecan pralines I have ever tasted. The year I was so busy cooking for parties I commissioned her to make some so I could give them away. I know that technically, that's cheating, so now that she has generously shared her recipe, I intend to get myself busy.

Another gift I always adore comes from my antiques-dealer friend Peter Patout. His Aunt Evelyn's candied kumquats are fabulous on cake or ice cream, with pork or duck or sweet potatoes, and I once slivered them and used them to decorate the top of a glamorous holiday charlotte russe. Peter managed to finagle Evelyn's recipe, which calls for three days of boiling and stirring—but only for a few minutes each morning. He says he actually enjoys the ritual of fooling with them while he makes his café au lait.

I plan to stir my own kumquat pot and I'll also be whipping up several batches of cake batter. There is no more elegant gift than a gorgeous cake, especially when you know someone is having a grand holiday dinner party. Mary makes an intense glazed lemon cake decorated with candied rind and fresh lemon leaves. A Lady Baltimore would also be fitting. But nothing invokes the season quite like a Red Velvet cake. When I was little I thought a Red Velvet cake was just about the most magical thing I'd ever seen. Creamy white icing is cut through to reveal moist layers of cake the color of Dorothy's slippers. I don't think I've ever been served one above the Mason-Dixon line, but according to *Great Desserts of the South*, the cake was imported from Manhattan. A "Southern lady" had a piece sometime in the late 1920s or early 1930s at the Waldorf-Astoria and asked for the recipe. The hotel gave it to her along with a hefty bill, which she paid, and then she shared the recipe with everyone she knew. If any of that is remotely true, I'm grateful to her. And I know it may be hokey to use whole bottles of red food coloring to color a cake, but I don't care. It looks fabulous, and it will be a refreshing change for my gifts to be in the red rather than my bank account.

EVELYN PATOUT'S PRESERVED KUMQUATS

*   *   *

1 quart kumquats

2 cups sugar

1½ cups light corn syrup

Scrub the kumquats thoroughly. Prick each several times with a large needle or poultry-trussing pin. Put them in a large saucepan and add water to cover. Bring to a boil, lower heat, and simmer, uncovered, for 10 minutes. Drain.

Combine the sugar and 3 cups of water in a large saucepan. Boil for 5 minutes. Add the kumquats and boil again. Remove from the heat and set aside, covered, overnight. The next morning, add ½ cup corn syrup. Bring to a boil, remove from heat, cover, and let stand overnight again. Repeat the process twice more.

On the fourth morning, after the kumquats have been brought to a boil, spoon them into hot, sterilized, Mason-type jars. Pour in the hot syrup to within ¼ inch of the top of each jar and seal. Refrigerate until ready to give or seal in a hot-water bath according to the jar manufacturer's directions and store.

NOTE: For directions on how to sterilize jars, see page 890 of the 75th anniversary edition of *Joy of Cooking*.

MARY COOPER'S PRALINES

YIELD: 2 DOZEN

. . .

1 cup firmly packed dark brown sugar

1 cup granulated sugar

½ cup evaporated milk

1 cup pecan halves or pieces

2 tablespoons butter

1½ teaspoons vanilla extract

In a deep, heavy, 2-quart saucepan, combine the brown sugar, granulated sugar, and milk and cook over medium heat, stirring constantly, until the sugars melt. Cook, stirring frequently to keep mixture from bubbling over, until a candy thermometer reads 228 degrees. Add the pecans and butter and stir until the butter melts. Continue cooking until the thermometer reaches 232 degrees. Remove from the heat and stir in the extract. Allow to cool, stirring occasionally, until the mixture loses some of its gloss.

Spoon the praline mixture onto parchment paper, forming 24 thin patties, each about 2 inches in diameter. Let cool at least a half hour. Wrap individually in wax-paper squares.

RED VELVET CAKE

* * *

FOR THE CAKE

Butter for greasing pans

2 cups all-purpose flour, plus
    extra for dusting the
    pans

1 tablespoon unsweetened
    cocoa powder

1 teaspoon salt

1½ cups sugar

½ cup vegetable shortening

2 eggs

1 cup buttermilk

1 teaspoon vanilla extract

2 bottles (1 ounce each)
    red food coloring

1 teaspoon baking soda

1 tablespoon white vinegar

FOR THE ICING

4 egg yolks

⅔ cup sugar

½ cup whole milk

16 tablespoons (2 sticks) unsalted butter, softened, plus
    additional if needed

1 tablespoon vanilla extract, bourbon, or rum

Chopped or halved pecans for decoration

To make the cake layers: Preheat the oven to 350 degrees. Butter and flour two 9-inch round cake pans. Combine the flour, cocoa, and salt in a sifter and sift three times to thoroughly mix in
cocoa powder. Using an electric mixer, beat the sugar with the
shortening until blended. Beat in the eggs one at a time, mixing
well after each addition. Beat another minute at medium speed.

    Alternately beat the flour mixture (in four parts) and the buttermilk (in three parts) into the sugar mixture. (Do not overbeat.) Add the extract and food coloring and mix well to color evenly. Dissolve the baking soda in the vinegar and quickly fold it into the batter. Pour half the batter into each prepared cake pan and bake until the cake top springs back when gently pressed, 20 to 25 minutes. Turn out the layers onto wire racks and let cool for 5 minutes.

To make the icing: Place the egg yolks in a large mixing bowl and gradually beat in the sugar with a whisk or mixer. Beat until the mixture is a thick, pale yellow and forms a ribbon when a spoonful is dropped on the surface. Heat the milk to almost boiling and beat into the egg mixture by droplets. Pour into a heavy saucepan and cook over medium heat, stirring with a wooden spoon until mixture is thick enough to lightly coat and spoon (about 165 degrees on a candy thermometer). Immediately set the pan in a basin of cold water and beat until the custard is barely tepid. Strain the custard into another bowl, and beat in the softened butter by spoonfuls. Beat in the flavoring. The icing should be smooth and thick. If it looks grainy or curdled, beat in additional softened butter, a teaspoonful at a time. Chill the icing until cold but still spreadable.

To assemble the cake: Place one cake layer on a serving plate, and spread some icing on top. Cover with the second layer, and spread the remaining icing over the top and sides of the cake. Sprinkle the top with chopped pecans, or press halved pecans around the top edge.

NOTE: The icing may be refrigerated for several days, or frozen for several weeks. To use, let stand at room temperature until it can be beaten to spreading consistency.

Eat the Rich Stuff

❖

O f all the Christmas images of my childhood, by far the most vivid is of the vast trunk of my grandparents' gray Cadillac filled with the bounty they brought to the Mississippi Delta from Nashville. Every other year they drove down to visit us for the holidays, and every other year I couldn't wait to see the car come up the driveway. (On off years, the same loot came on the bus.) There were always dozens of presents wrapped in silver-and-gold paper, an enormous country ham, a caramel cake, a chess pie, and a chocolate chess pie. But the thing I remember most was the plum pudding, bought from some mail-order place and tied up in yards of red cellophane with a huge silver ribbon. We never even ate it. The puddings piled up, still in their wrappings, on the top shelf of the coat closet, until one year I insisted we actually cook one. We all discovered that it was delicious. (Actually, we discovered that pretty much everything served with hard sauce is delicious.)

It has been a long time since I laid eyes on those glamorous red packages, and my grandparents are long dead. These days when I think of Christmas at home, I think first of cheese straws and roasted pecans. The pecans are roasted with butter and salt until they are gorgeous and golden with just the right crunch. And by cheese straws, I don't mean the ubiquitous and tasteless parmesan-coated, puff pastry twists found in every gourmet shop in Manhattan; I mean ridged rectangular wafers made of the heavenly combination of cheddar, butter, flour, and cayenne pepper that melts in your mouth and is best made with an old-fashioned cookie press. They're crunchy in texture, sharp in flavor; there is almost nothing I'd rather eat.

And there is plenty of opportunity. Every year tins of both cheese straws and pecans occupy a whole counter in my mother's kitchen, presents from various local cooks. They are passed on silver sandwich trays at every holiday party, pressed upon bearers of gifts, ranging from old friends to the beleaguered UPS man.

I think the reason they loom so large in my adult holiday memories is because they are almost always consumed with a drink. In *The Southern Hospitality Cookbook*, the author, Winifred Cheney, introduces two recipes for cheese straws with the information that they are "marvelous at a cocktail party" and "excellent with alcoholic beverages." Before offering her version of the pecans, she hastens to tell us that they, too, are "delicious to serve with any type of drink at any party."

I think we need more commentary like this in cookbooks and more space devoted to party fare, especially these days. I keep reading about the nation's desire for comfort food during these trying times, but I think it is far more comforting to entertain and be entertained by friends and family than to hunker down in sweats, as though in a bunker, munching on macaroni and cheese and meatloaf. Christmas is always a bit trying, what with shopping and relatives and the inevitable emotional outbursts (my best friend once had a small nervous breakdown in the middle of the Wal-Mart in our hometown). So even without Al Qaeda and the war and all manner of other bad news, I find it is generally helpful to make an extra effort to be festive. To that end, I always wear my silver lamé Manolo Blahnik mules with the chinchilla trim and, often, my Santa hat, a gift from my friend McGee. She bought us each one years ago to wear on our long drive home to the Delta, which makes my point again: it is important to enter into the exercise in the right spirit even if you look like a fool.

I never serve eggnog, the one holiday culinary tradition I have not been able to get behind, but I do make milk punch. With its frothy top and not-so-jaundiced color, a milk punch is prettier to look at than eggnog and is not nearly as rich and cloying, saved from that state by an effective combination of bourbon and brandy. They are especially good before a holiday lunch with, naturally, cheese straws and pecans. By evening, everyone wants a Santa hat. (When McGee and I stopped for gas on our drive that year, people actually offered us money for ours.)

Like funny hats, excess is often necessary. The first Christmas after 9/11, I hosted a Christmas Eve dinner party with another close friend from home, M.T. We grew up together; our fathers have been business partners for more than fifty years, and we love to cook together. So we offered a civilized meal to all the adults among our extended families and close friends who hadn't yet succumbed to the nesting syndrome, or who were not busy putting together Barbie's Dream House (some of those parents came in shifts). Jeremiah Tower, a great chef and a very smart man, once wrote, referring to the whole black truffles he shares with friends during the holidays, that "it is more interesting to listen to the rapturous sighs of others than of oneself." In that spirit, we served chateaubriand with black-truffle sauce as our main course, along with potatoes Anna and Julia Child's over-the-top gratinéed spinach Mornay.

We started our feast with caviar on blini brushed with melted butter and smeared with the tiniest bit of crème fraîche. Then we moved on to sautéed oysters on toast (I think you can never serve too many oysters over the holidays), and we ended with my old favorite, plum pudding. Then we raised our glasses to our physical and spiritual nourishment with the cognac we used to light the pudding. By then we were fully armed to face the evil lurking around us, not to mention the often stressful day ahead. It is always important to remember what Oscar Wilde said: "After a good dinner, one can forgive anybody, even one's own relatives."

CHEESE STRAWS

YIELD: 5 DOZEN

8 tablespoons (1 stick) butter, softened

6 ounces extra-sharp, grated cheddar cheese

2 ounces parmesan, freshly grated

½ teaspoon salt

½ teaspoon cayenne pepper (add a pinch more if you like
   them a bit hotter)

1½ cups all-purpose flour

Preheat the oven to 350 degrees. Mix the butter with the cheeses and the seasonings in a large bowl. Add the flour and knead into a smooth dough.

Pack the dough in batches into a cookie press and press through the flat, ridged-line opening onto an ungreased cookie sheet to form "straws" 2½ to 3 inches in length.

Bake the straws until golden (do not let them brown) and crisp, about 15 minutes. Remove from the pan with a metal spatula and let cool. Serve or store in an airtight container.

TOASTED PECANS

. . .

4 tablespoons (½ stick) butter, melted

4 cups pecan halves

1 tablespoon of salt

½ teaspoon cayenne or white pepper

Preheat the oven to 325 degrees. Place the butter and the pecans in a medium bowl and toss to coat.

Spread the pecans in one layer in a shallow baking pan or a cookie sheet and bake for 25 minutes. Shake the pan, stirring the nuts two or three times while baking to prevent scorching. Remove from the oven and let the pecans cool in the pan. Sprinkle with salt and cayenne or white pepper, tossing to coat. Serve or store in an airtight container.

SAUTÉED OYSTERS ON TOAST

YIELD: 6 SERVINGS

6 slices homemade white bread or Pepperidge Farm sandwich white
8 tablespoons (1 stick) butter, plus additional for toast
¼ cup chopped Serrano or prosciutto ham (about 1 ounce), thinly sliced and minced (Smithfield, or any good country ham, can be substituted)
⅓ cup finely chopped shallots
¼ cup finely chopped green bell pepper
1 pint shucked oysters (about 18 oysters), drained
Salt
Freshly ground black pepper
Dash of Tabasco sauce
Juice of 1 lemon (preferably a Meyer lemon)
Finely chopped flat-leaf parsley

To make the toast: Preheat the oven to 450 degrees. Trim the crusts from the bread and discard. Spread some softened butter on both sides of the bread slices. Place the bread slices on a cookie sheet and grill for 8 to 10 minutes, turning once so that both sides of the bread are golden brown.

Meanwhile, melt the 8 tablespoons of butter in a large heavy skillet over medium heat, add the ham and sauté for 2 to 3 minutes, until it is slightly crisp. Add the shallots and the bell pepper, turn the heat to low, and cook for another 2 minutes. Add the oysters and cook until they have plumped and are beginning to curl on the edges. Quickly swirl in salt and pepper to taste, the Tabasco and lemon juice. Spoon the oysters over the toasts, sprinkle with the chopped parsley, and serve.

MILK PUNCH

* * *

FOR THE SIMPLE SYRUP

1½ cups sugar

FOR THE PUNCH

2 quarts whole milk

1 quart vanilla ice cream or heavy cream

4 cups brandy

2 cups bourbon

1 tablespoon vanilla extract

Whole nutmeg

To make the simple syrup: Combine the sugar and ¾ cup of water in a saucepan and stir to dissolve the sugar. Heat over medium heat, stirring occasionally, until the mixture is boiling. Let simmer until the mixture is clear, about 8 minutes. Pour into a jar and cool. Refrigerate until cold.

To make the punch: Whisk the milk and the ice cream or the heavy cream together in a large pitcher or punch bowl until it is blended. Stir in the spirits and the extract and simple syrup to taste. Refrigerate until thoroughly chilled. To serve, pour into highball glasses and grate nutmeg on top.

NOTE: For individual cocktails, combine an ounce of brandy, an ounce of bourbon, an ounce of milk, a half ounce of cream, a half teaspoon of vanilla, and a teaspoon of simple syrup (or more to taste) in a shaker with ice. Shake vigorously, pour into a highball glass, and top with grated nutmeg.

Pump It Up

❁

When I want to bring the house down," my friend M.T. told me not long ago, "I make a soufflé. And when I really want to bring the house down, I make two." When she goes for the latter, she serves something like a rib roast with a cheese soufflé for the main course, and individual chocolate soufflés for dessert. "I mean you're mixing those egg whites, you might as well go on."

We were talking about the stuff that really impresses folks around a dinner table and feeling a little guilty because a soufflé is so damn easy. I remember a time before I knew this, when I was still in college and blown away by the sight of someone making a soufflé in his actual home. (As opposed to the old-fashioned French restaurants I'd been to, where the waiter would come out before you even ordered and ask if you'd like to have a chocolate or a Grand Marnier soufflé for dessert.) My host, D. Gorton, was a photographer for *The New York Times* who had lived all over the place, and he really knew how to cook. He passed around a basket of perfectly fried tiny whitebait for an hors d'oeuvre, made roast duck as an entrée, and then, at the end, he outdid himself with a raspberry and a chocolate soufflé. They were gorgeous, one a deep pink, the other a rich mahogany, both dusted with powdered sugar and barely shimmying in their dishes as they were brought out from the kitchen. More than twenty years have passed since then, and I have eaten and made a whole lot of soufflés, but I'm still impressed by the memory. M.T. is right—a soufflé is guaranteed to bring down the house.

In my own house, soufflés were not on the menu. My mother had plenty of dazzlers in her repertoire, but I never saw her whip up a soufflé. Maybe, like me, she thought they were too hard or too last-minute. In her soufflé dish she always put something called "mock cheese soufflé," a cheesy bread pudding that is really, really good—and beyond simple—but, as the name suggests, not a soufflé.

Anyway, soufflés are not hard—and they don't even have to be last-minute. The recipes for almost all of them, both sweet and savory, allow you to make the base as much as a day ahead of time, and to fold in the beaten egg whites just before baking. Julia Child swears you can even wait an hour after the whites have been added without doing any damage. Simply pour the batter into the dish and put an empty pot or kettle on top.

Only three things are really important in making a soufflé. First, the egg whites should be beaten until they are smooth and shiny and about seven times their volume, at which point they should hold stiff peaks. The best way to achieve this is with a standing mixer. (Snobs who tell you to beat the whites by hand with a wire whisk in a copper bowl only want to torture you—it is impossible to tell the difference.) Second, fold in those egg whites fast. Spend way less than a minute on the process or you will beat out the volume, which is the whole point. And finally, when it's done, get the soufflé to the table. You have a maximum of four or five minutes before it deflates. It will still taste swell, but you'll lose a bit of that crucial bringing-down-the-house factor.

Once you've got the hang of it, making soufflés is great fun. You can add almost anything to them: cold poached eggs hidden in the batter of a cheese soufflé make a soufflé Vendome; glacéed fruits soaked in kirsch transforms a vanilla soufflé into a soufflé Rothschild. Creamed or sautéed lobster, shrimp, or crabmeat is fabulous added to a cheese soufflé (I like cheddar best with crab), as is a bit of ground ham.

What I love about them the most is that they lend themselves to such creative menu combinations. The late, great Bill Blass, whose taste in food was as unerring as his taste in fashion, often served a cheese grits soufflé with crusty roast beef, and a sour-cream-and-chive soufflé (the recipe is in Nan Kempner's *R.S.V.P.*) with smoked salmon. A blue cheese soufflé is a perfect savory dessert when accompanied by pears poached in port. Two wonderfully versatile soufflés are the garlic soufflé and goat cheese soufflé from Alice Waters's *Chez Panisse Menu Cookbook*. I once served the goat cheese soufflé with a fresh ham and curried lentils, and the garlic is wonderful with leg of lamb.

Of course there are few combinations more elegant than a cheese soufflé with a green salad and a cold glass of white wine. When M.T. and I want to pretend like we have lives that we don't, we put on nice dresses and go to Manhattan's La Goulue or Payard, both of which have excellent versions of that exact menu. There's something very civilized and ladies lunch-y about it—in fact the first luncheon I ever gave consisted of my mother's mock cheese soufflé and a chicken salad with preserved ginger and mango that I'd found in *Vogue*. I invited some men to my lunch, but in *James Beard's Menus for Entertaining*, there's a chapter called "Ladies Only" in which one menu features a crab soufflé flavored with a bit of tomato paste and cognac (Beard loved cognac), and another has an apricot soufflé for dessert.

My favorite dessert soufflé is the lemon one I include here, and it's hard to beat any chocolate soufflé made with Valrhona chocolate. I think the next time that I, like my old friend D. Gorton, want to leave an indelible memory on an impressionable heart, I'll serve the lemon soufflé with whipped cream and a chocolate soufflé with a cold, coffee crème anglaise. The soufflés won't fall (if the egg whites are beaten stiff they never do), but, with any luck, the house will.

FRANÇOIS PAYARD'S CHOCOLATE UPSIDE-DOWN SOUFFLES

YIELD: 8 SERVINGS

Unsalted butter for greasing the soufflé cups, plus 1½
   sticks (6 ounces)
⅓ cup plus 1 tablespoon sugar, plus sugar for preparing the
   soufflé cups
6 ounces unsweetened chocolate, cut into small pieces
4 large eggs, separated
2 teaspoons fresh lemon juice
Whipped cream or vanilla ice cream for serving

Preheat the oven to 375 degrees. Butter eight 4-ounce soufflé
cups or ceramic ramekins and dust them with enough sugar to
completely coat the bottoms and sides.

Melt the 1½ sticks of butter over medium heat. Remove from
the heat and add the chocolate pieces. Stir with a whisk until the
chocolate is melted and smooth. Set aside.

Beat the egg yolks at medium speed with a mixer, gradually
adding the ⅓ cup sugar. Beat until thick and pale yellow, 5 to 6
minutes. Pour in the butter and chocolate mixture and mix at low
speed just until blended, making sure the chocolate mixture is well
incorporated.

Using clean beaters, beat the egg whites in a separate bowl until foamy, then add the lemon juice, and continue beating until
soft peaks form. Add the remaining tablespoon of sugar and beat
until the peaks are stiff and shiny. Stir one-fourth of the egg whites
into the chocolate mixture. Gently fold in the rest and spoon into
the prepared cups. Set the cups in a baking pan.

Place the pan in the oven and pour in boiling water until it reaches 1 inch up the sides of the cups. Bake the soufflés 10 to 15 minutes, until the top is firm and a knife inserted near the center comes out almost clean. Remove the pan from the oven and the cups from the pan. Let the soufflés sit for 2 minutes.

Invert the cups onto individual dessert plates and unmold the soufflés. Top with whipped cream or vanilla ice cream.

MOCK CHEESE SOUFFLÉ

* * *

Softened butter for greasing the dish and buttering the
    bread

8 slices white sandwich bread, crusts removed

1 pound sharp cheddar cheese, grated

4 large eggs, beaten

½ teaspoon salt

2 cups whole milk

2 teaspoons Worcestershire sauce

Dash of cayenne pepper

Butter an 8-cup soufflé dish.

Butter each slice of bread on one side and cut into four squares.
Layer half the bread, buttered side up, in the bottom of the dish.
Cover with half the grated cheese. Repeat. Put the remaining ingredients in a bowl and mix well. Pour the mixture over the bread
and cheese, cover with plastic wrap, and refrigerate overnight.

Preheat the oven to 350 degrees. Uncover the soufflé and bake
on the center rack until the top is browned and the soufflé is bubbling around the edges, about 45 minutes.

LEMON SOUFFLÉ

YIELD: 4 SERVINGS

. . .

Softened butter for greasing the dish

5 tablespoons granulated sugar

1 cup milk

3 large egg yolks

1 tablespoon vanilla extract

¼ cup all-purpose flour

2 tablespoons finely grated lemon zest

4 tablespoons fresh lemon juice

1 tablespoon confectioners' sugar, plus more for sprinkling

5 large egg whites

Lightly whipped cream or cold crème anglaise for serving

Preheat the oven to 400 degrees. Butter an 8-cup soufflé dish and dust the bottom and sides with 2 tablespoons of the granulated sugar, shaking out the excess.

Heat the milk to boiling in a heavy saucepan. Remove from the heat. Whisk the egg yolks, extract, and 1 tablespoon of the granulated sugar until well blended, then whisk in the flour. Whisk in the hot milk in a thin, steady stream and blend until smooth. Return the mixture to the saucepan and cook over medium-low heat, stirring constantly, until the mixture is very thick, about 2 minutes. Remove from the heat.

Mix the lemon zest, lemon juice, and 1 tablespoon confectioners' sugar in a cup and whisk into the egg-yolk mixture. (At this point, the soufflé base can be refrigerated, covered with plastic wrap pressed directly on its surface, for up to a day.) If the soufflé base is still warm, whisk briefly until smooth. If made in advance and refrigerated, place it over low heat, whisk until just warm, and remove from the heat.

Beat the egg whites until soft peaks form. Sprinkle in the remaining 2 tablespoons granulated sugar and beat until stiff and shiny. Fold one-fourth of the whites into the soufflé base. Gently fold in the rest, being careful not to deflate the mixture. A few white streaks may remain.

Turn the mixture into the prepared dish and place on the center rack in the oven. Immediately reduce the oven temperature to 375 degrees. Bake until the soufflé is puffed and brown, 20 to 25 minutes; it should still wobble a bit. Sprinkle confectioners' sugar over the top and serve immediately with lightly whipped cream or very cold crème anglaise.

Party of One

❖

Jim Harrison, the great poet, novelist, food writer, and cook, once wrote a poem called "The Theory and Practice of Rivers," in which he describes his activities on the most overrated night of the year:

> On New Year's Eve I'm wrapped
> in my habits, looking up to the TV
> to see the red ball, the apple,
> rise or fall, I forget which:
> a poem on the cherry-wood table, a fire,
> a blizzard, some whiskey, three
> restless cats, and two sleeping dogs,
> at home and making three gallons
> of menudo for the revelers who'll
> need it come tomorrow after amateur night:
> about ten pounds of tripe, ancho,
> molida, serrano, and chipotle pepper, cumin,
> coriander, a few calves' or piglets' feet.
> I don't wonder what is becoming
> to the man already becoming.

Those are just a few lines of a very long and very beautiful poem, but I think I may love them the most because I always wanted to live them. How wonderful to be in that kitchen, with the pungent smells of the restorative menudo, the restless cats and great sleeping dogs. (Harrison's beloved English setter, Tess, would probably have been among them in the mid-80s when the poem was written). Not to mention a fire and some whiskey instead of the usual—and usually bad—New Year's Eve party champagne.

It sounds so good, in fact, that I have made my New Year's resolution ahead of time. Next year I, too, will be standing in my kitchen with the TV silent on the counter and a pot simmering on the stove. Instead of false eyelashes and five-inch Manolo Blahniks, I will don my favorite ancient pullover, an apron, and some Keds. Like Harrison, I will sip a modest whiskey and prepare some suitable sustenance for the next day's onslaught of queasy amateurs. But instead of menudo, I'll make black-eyed peas stewed with ham hocks, a dish that, in most parts of the South, is said to bring you luck and prosperity for the rest of the year. Finally, I even have a dog for the occasion.

Harrison is hardly the first person to refer to New Year's Eve as amateur night, the night when everybody goes out and gets way too drunk because it is the only way really to survive the great pressure of having to have a fabulous New Year's Eve. With maybe two or three exceptions I have never had a good time at a New Year's Eve party, including my own. I much prefer the year I stayed home, alone, and paid bills and wrote letters to everyone I'd been meaning to write all year long (and the year before that). I'm pretty sure I had a delicious can of Campbell's chicken noodle soup with buttered toast, and a celebratory Scotch and water toward the end of the evening.

I also enjoyed the New Year's Eve before the Clinton impeachment trial, which I spent writing a profile of Trent Lott for *Newsweek*. Now I realize that's not everybody's idea of a good time, but I felt virtuous, productive, sober. At one point an old flame called to wish me a Happy New Year; at another I walked around the corner to the party my friend Brobson Lutz gives every year. On his dining room table there was a huge glass bowl containing at least two pounds of osetra caviar, my favorite. I ate an embarrassing amount and then, at eleven, I walked back home. It was a perfect evening.

I must say that most evenings involving caviar are pretty perfect, even if you have to dress up and go out to get it. The beauty of staying home alone is that you can have it all to yourself, eating it straight out of the tin with a horn spoon. But when company comes I usually serve it with blini, which is what I did the night of the most high–pressure New Year's Eve ever, in 1999, the night before the start of the new millenium (unless you are one of those sticklers who think that the year everybody should have celebrated like mad was the night before 2001).

My friend and former New Orleans neighbor Jaston Williams threw an elaborate masked ball, and I gave a dinner party for some of the revelers at my house beforehand. It was, against all odds, a fabulous night. Jaston, one of the writers and stars of the hilarious "Greater Tuna" plays, is as extraordinarily creative and generous as a host as he is a playwright and actor. All week, tango lessons had been available to guests who might want to stick a rose in their teeth. Packages filled with masks and gorgeous handblown Venetian glass beads were delivered. Thus prompted, we rose to the occasion and dressed, per the instructions on the invitation, in black-and-white evening clothes. We drank vodka and (very good) champagne and ate corn blini topped with salmon caviar and buckwheat blini topped with osetra. (My friend Byron Seward, a cotton farmer and generous wine connoisseur who brought the champagne, recommends Pol Roger "Winston Churchill," or, of course, Krug, if you can afford it, to stand up to the caviar. But he says that a yeasty and more moderately priced Roederer Brut will also do the job.) We then sat down to a stomach-coating dinner of a Provençal daube (from *Patricia Wells At Home in Provence*), cheese grits soufflé, crusty French bread, and a romaine salad with red onion and avocado and a lemony vinaigrette. Byron supplied a Vieux Télégraphe Chateauneuf-du-Pape and a robust Nuits-Saint-Georges. I could have stopped right there, but we tied on our masks and put on our beads and made our way through the French Quarter to Jaston's beautiful ball, where we felt more as if we were in Venice at carnival than in New Orleans on New Year's Eve.

The next morning, we ate leftover daube for breakfast and looked forward to a late lunch of lucky black-eyed peas and rice. I have no idea where this tradition came from, but the dish itself originated with the slaves who were brought to work the rice fields of the Carolinas, where the mixture of rice and beans simmered together is called "Hoppin' John." In New Orleans, black-eyed peas are often cooked with sausage in addition to the ubiquitous ham hock and served separately over rice. They're usually accompanied by a side dish of cabbage by people who really want to hedge their bets. The cabbage, they say, signifies greenbacks.

BUCKWHEAT BLINI

YIELD: ABOUT 6 DOZEN

, , ,

1½ cups whole milk

4 tablespoons unsalted
   butter, plus extra for
   cooking the blini and
   serving

1 teaspoon sugar

2 teaspoons active dry
   yeast

3 large eggs, separated

1 cup all-purpose flour

1 cup buckwheat flour

1 teaspoon salt

8 ounces crème fraîche or
   sour cream

3 ounces caviar, preferably
   osetra

Heat the milk and the 4 tablespoons of butter over low heat until the butter is melted, and let cool slightly. Meanwhile, combine the sugar and 2 tablespoons of warm water and stir to dissolve the sugar. Sprinkle the yeast over the sugar water and let stand in a warm place until the yeast is frothy, about 5 minutes. Pour in the milk mixture, add the egg yolks, and whisk to blend.

Combine the flours and salt and gradually whisk into the yeast mixture until smooth. Cover the bowl tightly with plastic wrap, and let the batter rise in a warm place until doubled in bulk, about 1 hour.

Stir to deflate the batter. (The batter can be covered and refrigerated for 24 hours before proceeding.) Beat the egg whites until soft peaks form. Gently fold the whites into the batter just until blended.

Preheat the oven to 200 degrees. Melt enough butter to coat the bottom of a large griddle or skillet over medium to medium-high heat. When the butter sizzles, drop tablespoons of batter onto the surface to make blini roughly 2 inches in diameter. Cook until bubbles appear on the tops and the bottoms are golden brown. Turn and cook until the bottom of the blini are lightly browned. Place the blini, overlapping but not stacked (they will get soggy), on a baking sheet and keep warm in the oven while cooking the remaining batter. Stop using the batter when bubbles no longer appear on the top (there may be about 1 cup left), or the blini will be thin and tough.

To serve, brush the blini lightly with melted butter and top each with a dab of crème fraîche or sour cream and a small dollop of caviar.

NOTE: Blini may be made ahead, wrapped well, and frozen. To thaw, place on a baking sheet, cover loosely with aluminum foil, and heat in a 350-degree oven until warm, about 10 minutes.

BLACK-EYED PEAS WITH ANDOUILLE SAUSAGE AND RICE

Adapted from Hot Links and Country Flavors,
by Bruce Aidells and Denis Kelly

YIELD: 6 TO 8 SERVINGS

* * *

2 cups dried black-eyed
    peas, or 4 cups fresh or
    frozen
1½ pounds andouille
    sausage or other good-
    quality smoked sausage
¼ pound chunk country or
    smoked ham
6 cups chicken stock or
    water
1 tablespoon bacon grease
    or olive oil
1 medium onion, finely
    chopped

1 celery rib, finely chopped
1 tablespoon minced garlic
3 sprigs fresh thyme or 1½
    teaspoons dried thyme
2 bay leaves
½ teaspoon pickling spices
1 or 2 dried chile peppers
    or 1 teaspoon freshly
    ground black pepper
Salt
4 cups cooked rice
Chopped scallions, Tabasco
    sauce, and cider vinegar
    for serving

If using dried peas, rinse and soak the peas overnight in water to cover by 3 inches. Drain and place in a 6- to 8-quart pot with a ½-pound piece of the andouille, the ham, and the stock. Heat to boiling, then reduce to a simmer. (If using fresh or frozen peas, boil the stock first, then add peas, the ½-pound piece of andouille, and the ham. Return to a boil, then reduce to a simmer.)

Heat the bacon grease or oil in a heavy skillet, add the onion and celery, and cook until soft. Add to the peas along with the garlic and the herbs, spices, and seasonings. Simmer the dried peas for 2 to 2½ hours; fresh or frozen for 30 to 45 minutes. In both cases, the peas should be tender and the liquid should begin to thicken.

Slice the remaining sausage into ½-inch rounds. Fry briefly in a nonstick skillet and add to the peas. Remove the whole piece of sausage and the ham and chop roughly; return them to the pot. Cook for another 15 minutes. Remove the thyme sprigs, bay leaves, and chile pods.

To serve: Ladle the pea mixture over the rice and sprinkle with chopped scallions, Tabasco, and vinegar to taste.

PART II
CHEFS I'VE KNOWN

Panning Out

❁

O ne of the many things I like about my friend James Villas is that he is not a snob. The esteemed cookbook author and former food writer for *Town & Country* was a Fulbright scholar, clocked many an hour at the great Le Pavillon, and celebrated his fiftieth birthday with a party at Le Cirque attended by one hundred chefs, restaurateurs, and friends (including Pierre Franey, who designed the menu). But he is also from North Carolina, loves his mama (with whom he has collaborated on three cookbooks), and knows the value of a good casserole. In fact, he has written a book about them, *Crazy for Casseroles*, in which he asserts that they "remain one of America's greatest contributions to world gastronomy" and that they "will undoubtedly still be around long after much of today's phony novelty has been burned to a crisp."

I agree. I have to, really—casseroles were staples in my house when I was a child, and now I make them myself, all the time. Among my mother's wedding presents were several footed silver holders for two-and-three-quart Pyrex casserole dishes, and all her friends have them, too. They are forever making casseroles and toting them to the sick and the grieving, to parties and church suppers, to the freezer just to have on hand. They make them for breakfast and dessert; and they keep track of their dishes by writing their names on masking tape on the bottoms. My mother's best friend, Bossy, can generally be counted on for Chicken Wiggle, a combination of chicken, noodles, peas, pimentos, mushrooms, and cream of mushroom soup. Bossy took it to New Orleans from Mississippi when her oldest daughter, Elizabeth, had her first child—much to the horror of Elizabeth's husband, who was a very good, and very sophisticated, cook. He should have tried it. Chicken Wiggle is delicious. There are very few versions of chicken spaghetti casseroles that are not. Craig Claiborne (who was from Indianola, Mississippi) made his mother's version once a year for a dozen close friends in East Hampton and included it in at least one cookbook.

Claiborne's recipe is also in Villas's book—he calls it "a masterpiece of casserole art"—as is another famous noodle casserole, Johnny Marzetti. In *The Party*, Sally Quinn gives the recipe for her mother's version (spelled "Johnny Mazetti") and tells the story of the time she borrowed her mother's electric casserole cooker to make it at her tiny Dupont Circle apartment in Washington. She'd invited all sorts of grand people over—Fleur Cowles, Ambassador David Bruce and his wife, Evangeline—but unfortunately forgot to plug in the casserole. By the time she remembered, and the casserole was at last done, everybody was drunk, and, according to Quinn, David Bruce was trying to make out with Barbara Howar in her bedroom. It was, she writes, "the best party I've ever had."

Everybody has casserole memories. The other day I asked my husband to name his favorite casserole and he didn't miss a beat: "tuna noodle with crushed potato chips on top." He hasn't eaten it in more than thirty years, but his aunt's cook used to make it for him two or three times a week, and I guess I should break down and do the same. My mother did not make tuna noodle casserole (although Stouffer's did, and I ate plenty of it in college, along with those other outstanding Stouffer's creations, like Turkey Tetraz-zini). She made (and still makes) an excellent lasagna, two differ-ent squash casseroles, eggplant parmesan, an eggplant-and-shrimp casserole, three kinds of spinach casseroles, and a swanky casserole of oysters, chicken, shrimp, mushrooms, cream, and sherry that she must have served at more than a hundred dinner parties in the 70s.

Christmas at our house is a veritable festival of casseroles—there are so many there is not enough room for them on the side-board and the dining room table together, so we have to make a lap through the kitchen in order to serve our plates. There is sweet po-tato (of course—though now that we are old and I have thrown a fit, she no longer tops it with marshmallows), broccoli and cheese, scalloped oysters, baked apricots (for years it was the only thing one of my brothers would eat), and cornbread dressing. But sadly, no string-bean casserole topped with canned Durkee fried onion rings, a holiday classic that is my favorite guilty pleasure.

I was determined to make it myself one Thanksgiving a few years ago when a group of friends and I cooked together at a house we bor-rowed in Connecticut. But when it was time to get started I discov-ered someone had done away with the two cans of fried onions I'd brought with me from New York. She still denies it, but I am con-vinced it was my friend M.T., who has been to cooking school in France several times and has maybe gotten a little too big for her Mississippi britches. I got her point about not wanting to mar the general beauty and upscale nature of our table, but I bet that casse-role would have gone over a lot bigger than the brussels sprouts we served instead. I myself am not above cooking with Durkee or even canned soups—Villas provides several recipes with canned soups (it would be hard not to), including one from M.F.K. Fisher.

As with most things, however, there is a class system at work here.

With apologies to my husband, I have to say that topping a casserole with crushed potato chips hovers dangerously close to the low-class zone, but the chips are not nearly as bad as crushed cornflakes. (When I get around to making him a tuna noodle casserole I am going to make like Stouffer's and Villas and go with buttered bread crumbs.) I'm not sure where I'd rank crumbled Pepperidge Farm herbed stuffing mix, but saltine crumbs fall safely in the middle-class category. My mother tops almost all her casseroles with crushed Ritz crackers, which, naturally, I place in the highest class. Here, I include her spinach-and-artichoke casserole covered in them.

Many people might quarrel with this particular dish being dubbed high class, as every main ingredient comes from a box, can, or package. But she has served it to diplomats and even a famous Manhattan hostess with great success, and more important, it takes about ten minutes to put together. Once, in a fit of high-mindedness, I made another spinach-and-artichoke casserole that I cobbled together out of two recipes from *Mastering the Art of French Cooking*. It had: fresh artichoke bottoms, blanched and braised in butter; fresh spinach, blanched, braised, and creamed; and a Mornay sauce made with both Gruyère and Parmesan cheeses (as opposed to the Cheez Whiz and Velveeta that pervade Junior League cookbooks). It took forever to make and was really rich and really good, but I still love my mother's just as much. I've also included Villas's seafood lasagna, which, when you think about it, is just a more expensive (and arguably more delicious) version of tuna-noodle casserole. I got raves when I last served it, but then most people rave about casseroles. As Villas says: "If there's ever been anyone (food elitists included) whose basic instincts and appetite couldn't be sparked by the sight, aroma, and taste of a great casserole, I've yet to meet such an individual."

SEAFOOD LASAGNA

Adapted from Crazy for Casseroles, *by James Villas*

YIELD: 6 SERVINGS

. . .

4 tablespoons butter

½ pound fresh shrimp, boiled, shelled, and chopped

½ pound lump crabmeat

6 lasagna noodles

1 medium onion, finely chopped

½ pound fresh mushrooms, thinly sliced

1 tablespoon fresh lemon juice

Salt

Freshly ground black pepper

3 large eggs, beaten

2 cups half-and-half

¼ cup freshly grated Parmesan cheese

¾ cup shredded mozzarella cheese

Preheat the oven to 350 degrees. Butter a shallow 2-quart casserole with 1 tablespoon butter.

Combine the shrimp and crab in a large mixing bowl and toss well.

Bring a large pot of salted water to a boil, and cook the noodles, according to the package directions, until just tender. Drain and set aside.

Melt the remaining 3 tablespoons of butter in a large skillet, add the onion and mushrooms, and cook, stirring until softened, about 5 minutes. Add the onion mixture and lemon juice to the seafood. Season with salt and pepper to taste and toss again.

Combine the eggs, half-and-half, and Parmesan in another large bowl and stir until well blended. Add about two-thirds of the egg mixture to the seafood mixture, and stir again to mix well.

Spread about one-third of the seafood mixture over the bottom of the prepared casserole. Cover with 2 of the noodles, then spread another third of the mixture over the noodles; cover with 2 more noodles, and spread the remaining mixture over the top. Cover with the last 2 noodles, pour the remaining egg mixture over the noodles, and sprinkle the mozzarella evenly over the top. Bake in the center of the oven until bubbly and golden, about 35 minutes. Let stand 10 minutes before serving.

NOTE: Any poached and flaked white fish, or a mix of salmon and white fish, may be substituted for the shrimp and crabmeat.

SPINACH-AND-
ARTICHOKE CASSEROLE

YIELD: 6 TO 8 SERVINGS

* * *

1 tablespoon butter for greasing the baking dish
　½ cup butter, melted, plus 1 tablespoon, melted, for
　the topping
Two 10-ounce packages frozen chopped spinach
One 8-ounce package cream cheese, softened
1 teaspoon fresh lemon juice
One 14-ounce can artichoke hearts, drained and quartered
½ cup coarse Ritz cracker crumbs (about 10 crackers)

Preheat the oven to 350 degrees. Butter a shallow 2-quart casserole.

Cook the spinach according to the package directions, drain well, and place in a mixing bowl. Add the ½ cup of melted butter, the cream cheese, and the lemon juice and blend well with a fork.

Scatter the artichoke quarters evenly over the bottom of the greased casserole. Cover with the spinach mixture and smooth the top.

Cover the top with the Ritz crumbs, drizzle with the 1 tablespoon melted butter, and bake on the middle rack until bubbly in the center and lightly browned on the top, about 25 minutes. Cool for about 5 minutes and serve.

Getting Personal

❁

In *The Alice B. Toklas Cook Book*, the author tells of cooking for Picasso, a frequent guest at the house that she and Gertrude Stein shared in Paris. A finicky eater, he was on a medically supervised "diet" that forbade red meat or chicken but not, somehow, veal and mutton—or spinach soufflés. (Once, when Toklas tried to make a soufflé appear "less nourishing" by serving it with three different sauces, the artist pronounced her efforts a "cruel enigma.")

He also ate fish, so for a special lunch she poached "a fine striped bass" and decorated it in a way she hoped might "amuse" the great man. After she'd covered it with mayonnaise, she used a pastry tube full of more mayonnaise (dyed red this time with tomato paste) to make a design, along with the sieved whites and yolks of hard-boiled eggs, chopped herbs, and black truffles. "I was proud of my chef d'oeuvre," she writes, and Picasso did manage to comment on its beauty. But then he asked, "Should it not rather have been made in honor of Matisse than of me?"

I have tailored only two menus so specifically to my guests of honor, and I am happy to report that both were far more gracious.

The first was for my friend Robert Harling, the screenwriter of *Steel Magnolias* and *The First Wives Club*, among many others, and it was born of desperation. On my fortieth birthday, Bobby had given me no less than twelve gifts (for the twelve days of my birthday, a custom that, sadly, did not catch on among my other friends and family), numbered in the order that I was to open them and accompanied by sweet and hilarious notes on postcards that hinted at what was inside. And what was inside was always the most fabulous thing—usually something we had seen together that he knew I wanted, or something that perfectly filled some need in my life I didn't know I had. I was touched and thrilled but also not just a little flipped out—what in the world was I going to do for Bobby's birthday?

And then it hit me. He had given me a gorgeous lamp entirely encrusted with seashells, and one day, in one of my favorite shops, Ruzzetti & Gow, I saw some equally gorgeous silver seashell place-card holders. I bought a dozen, wrote his name on a card I stuck in one of them, wrapped them all up and enclosed a handwritten menu with courses inspired by the movies Bobby had written. The two of us spend pretty much all our time together eating, so it seemed fitting. Also, among my gifts were sixteen silver sauce spoons and about five sets of Laguiole steak knives; maybe he meant to encourage me.

Dessert was the easiest—he had just finished script-doctoring the first *Charlie's Angels*, so, of course, we had to have Charlie's Angel Cake, a delicious angel food cake layered with lemon curd and whipped cream from Maida Heatter's *Best Dessert Book Ever*. Since one of my favorite lines in *Steel Magnolias* is Dolly Parton's unforgettable declaration, "I haven't left the house without Lycra on these thighs since I was fourteen," I devised an hors d'oeuvre called Duck Rolls Dolly. Duck thighs (legs, too—I used duck confit from D'Artagnan) were diced and mixed with a little chili oil and Chinese five-spice powder, along with some cabbage, scallions, and ginger that had been sautéed in sesame oil. The mixture was then encased not in Lycra but rice-paper wrappers with melted pepper jelly for dipping. After that we had Crab Cakes Celeste (during most of *Soapdish*, Celeste—Sally Field—is extremely crabby), accompanied by Sauce Aurora (Aurora is Shirley MacLaine's character in *The Evening Star*, and there is, in fact, a French tomato-based sauce called Aurore, which we all scraped up with our sauce spoons).

I had to use the knives, of course, so I resorted to First Knives Club Rib-Eye Roast—corny, I know, but rescued by a sophisticated potato terrine, layered with a sliced white truffle, which I decided was the perfect stand-in for *The Evening Star*. I tossed the salad afterward with roasted pecans from Bobby's plantation in Natchitoches, Louisiana, and served it with wedges of artisanal Louisiana cheeses, which happen to be very good.

I think I may have had more fun making up the menu than we did eating it, which is the thing about these kinds of dinners. You can be playful or extravagant, you can be artistic, or you can indulge in bad puns, as I did for Bobby. No matter what, you have a point of departure. A few years ago, for example, when my good friend André Leon Talley published his memoir, *A.L.T.*, Catie Marron gave a lunch and she took as her guide the dishes of Talley's grandmother that are so lovingly described in the book. André is from North Carolina, and I am from Mississippi. Neither of us ever expected to be sitting in a swanky Park Avenue apartment eating astonishingly good versions of the food of our childhood: chicken hash with slivers of country ham, melt-in-your-mouth biscuits, the best lemon meringue pie I've ever tasted.

In the back of *The Chez Panisse Menu Cookbook*, Alice Waters reprints some of the restaurant's most memorable menus, and most of them, too, were inspired by people. A birthday dinner for a triple Scorpio featured "dark, savory flavors" and dishes that were "extremely esoteric but appealing," in keeping with the traits of the birth sign. An "exotic friend" got dishes inspired by *Les Diners de Gala*, by Salvador Dalí. A friend from New Orleans got boudin blanc and crab-and-corn bisque and Paul Prudhomme's filet of beef with debris gravy, while one who loved Provençal food was treated to tabbouleh, fish poached in stock with garlic and croutons, and leg of lamb with flageolets. My favorite menu was the one created for a Baudelaire society, using the names of Baudelaire's poems. "Le Mort Joyeux" was interpreted as a whole roast pigeon with the head still attached on a bed of black trumpet mushrooms; "Les Bijoux" was a salad with endive and "jewels" of fresh pink grapefruit.

It was in this spirit that I tackled my next birthday menu challenge, for my good friend Patrick Dunne. It was a big birthday for Patrick, so big that he declared it a jubilee, so the stakes were high. Fortunately, I had creative cohosts, Byron and Cameron Seward, because ours was to be one celebration of many. Also, Patrick, who owns the divine culinary antiques store Lucullus, in New Orleans, has unassailable taste, and he knows everything about food and how to serve it. Not only is his shop named after the great Roman gourmand, but he also has a wonderful collection of esoteric cookbooks and even wrote his own book, *The Epicurean Collector*. I knew we'd have to rise to the occasion, which actually made it more fun, as did the fact that Patrick would get all the references.

Because he grew up eating Southern country food in Corpus Christi, Texas, has an apartment in France where he buys the majority of his pieces, and loves the Creole cooking of his adopted home, New Orleans, we had a wide range of cuisines to play with. He loves oysters, so we passed fried ones as hors d'oeuvres, as well as Diana Kennedy's excellent rendition of "Mexican" marinated poached oysters that were served on pumpernickel toast points spread with a lime butter. For the first course, I made an old-fashioned crab stew. Then, since Patrick's favorite thing in life is corn pudding, I cooked individual ones, drizzled an intense shellfish reduction around the plates and, to gild the lily, passed heaping platters of fried green tomatoes around the table. After that we had two rémoulades—a red spicy Louisiana shrimp rémoulade and a white creamy French celery root one. Next, we managed to eat a boned rolled leg of lamb with braised fennel, followed by a salad with a walnut oil vinaigrette accompanied by French cheeses. I figured if Lucullus was known for his epic feasts, we should have one, too.

Cameron made some beautiful madeleines for dessert, which we piled high on a porcelain platter to accompany something neither of us could resist, Alice B. Toklas's Cream Perfect Love. The name alone is reason enough to serve it, but it is also the best Bavarian cream I've ever had. We chilled it in a wonderful old French copper mold that we borrowed, naturally, from Lucullus, and surrounded it with a macédoine of fruit. Patrick adored it, as we knew he would. In fact, he raved about the whole thing. Which is the real best reason to plan these menus. I only wish the long-suffering Alice could have lived to hear the praise.

CREAM PERFECT LOVE

Adapted from The Alice B. Toklas Cook Book

∘ ∘ ∘

1 cup milk

4 whole cloves

4 egg yolks

1 cup sugar

1 tablespoon unflavored gelatin

Vegetable oil or nonstick cooking spray

1½ cups heavy cream

Grated zest of 1 lemon

Assorted berries or cut fresh fruit for serving

Heat the milk and the cloves in a saucepan over low heat until hot.

Combine the egg yolks and sugar in a bowl and beat until lemon-colored. Slowly beat in the warm milk and cloves, and pour the custard in the top of a double boiler placed over simmering water. Stir with a wooden spoon until the custard is hot and coats the back of the spoon, about 15 minutes. Remove from heat, strain into a mixing bowl, and let cool slightly.

Meanwhile, place the gelatin in a small dish and add 1¼ cups cold water. Set aside to let it bloom, about 5 minutes. Stir the gelatin into the custard and continue to stir constantly until the gelatin is completely dissolved and the custard has cooled. (For rapid cooling, place the bowl of custard in a larger bowl of ice water.)

Lightly grease a 5-cup mold or bowl with oil or nonstick cooking spray. Place the heavy cream in a deep bowl and whip until the peaks are firm but not stiff. Fold the lemon zest and then the whipped cream into the custard. Pour into the prepared mold and refrigerate until firm.

When ready to serve, pull the custard away from the sides of the mold with your thumb to break the suction, invert onto a serving dish, and remove the mold. Surround with the macédoine of fruit.

Friendly Persuasion

❖

During the holiday season, generally marked by thick tension, high drama, and mini nervous breakdowns, we would all do well to take some lessons from the exemplary lives of Lee Bailey and Mary Cantwell. Bailey, who died in 2003 at the age of seventy-six, was the author of eighteen books on food and entertaining, a sort of lifestyle guru before there was such a thing, and the antithesis of Martha Stewart. "I really am too lazy to make radish roses, even if I liked them," he wrote in the introduction to *City Food,* where he also explained why the coconut flan on page 33 of his book was photographed showing the crack where it had been put back together. "I wanted you to see that it is the overall presentation that is important and that a few imperfections are perfectly acceptable."

Cantwell, who died in 2000 at sixty-nine, was the author of three memoirs and a member of the editorial board of the *New York Times,* but I knew her best as the witty features writer of my adolescent bible, *Mademoiselle,* and later as the author of that magazine's *Eat* column. Like Bailey, she loved food and cooking, but she was not a "foodie." In one article, she wrote that she had gone to the new culinary mecca of Napa Valley and that her "happiest meal" there included chili. Her recipes sounded like a good friend telling you how to do it: "Keep mushing it down with a wooden spoon and cook until you get a thickish sauce" were among the instructions for linguine with anchovies. "Toss everything together with a vinaigrette," she would say, assuming that anyone reading the column would know how to make one.

I never met either of these two, but I felt as if I knew them—well. I knew, for example, that Bailey had great taste—long before I opened one of his books, I would take the train from Washington to New York and ogle the incredibly chic items in his housewares boutique at Henri Bendel (when the store was still on 57th Street and very, very cool). When I did read his books, I could tell he was Southern just by looking at the pictures of lima beans in brown butter and cornbread cooked in a skillet. I didn't read Cantwell's excellent memoirs until after she died, but I knew from her food columns that she had a cat named Calypso, that her grandmother lived to be at least 103, and that she worked hard and reared two daughters and managed to bring a lot of joy into people's lives, including my own, with her cooking.

Cantwell wrote her column in the late 1970s, the same years I moved into my first college apartment and began cooking for my roommates and entertaining friends, including my *Newsweek* colleagues (well, not colleagues exactly, since I was the girl who answered the phone and clipped the newspapers), whom I was desperately trying to impress. Cantwell helped take the anxiety out of that process, explaining in her straightforward way how to make sophisticated (to me, anyway) dishes like veal chops with cream and endive, or a soufflé using nothing but eggs, sugar, and frozen lemonade.

Under Cantwell's tutelage, I became everybody's darling. "Jules," my roommate Nora would say almost every afternoon when I answered the phone by plugging a cord into our ancient switchboard ("Good afternoon, Washington bureau"), "if you cook tonight, I'll go to the grocery store."

Fortunately, our grocery store was the fabulous Neam's in Georgetown, where pristine heads of endive, bushy watercress, and tiny haricots verts were lined up in the produce department and the butcher would cut the most beautiful pieces of meat I had ever seen. Even more fortunately, Nora was possessed of her very generous father's American Express gold card, so I would whip up Cantwell's Filet Mignon with Roquefort or her Rock Cornish Game Hen with Tarragon on a Bed of Watercress. My life then, now that I think about it, was far more civilized than it is now.

By the time I moved into my second apartment, with a cat this time instead of roommates, Bailey's first cookbook, *Country Weekends*, had come out, and I learned that even large-scale entertaining could be relatively stress-free. I had grown up looking at the overwrought photographs in *Gourmet* magazine, in which the food did not look exactly edible and radish roses abounded. Bailey freed us from all that, showing not only the cracked flan but also flower "arrangements" that were relaxed bouquets in pitchers or the revolutionary notion of a glass cylinder filled with nothing but, say, anemones. Long before the nation became obsessed with all things regional and seasonal, he recommended simple dishes like fresh ripe figs for dessert and peaches dressed with lemon juice and cayenne pepper as a main-course accompaniment.

"Running a meal like clockwork is not one of his priorities," wrote Amy Gross in her foreword to *Country Weekends*, adding that Bailey rarely called people to dinner before 10 P.M. But in his company no one seemed to care—guests munched on pistachios or peanuts (virtually the only hors d'oeuvres he ever produced), made their own drinks, and wandered in and out of the kitchen, where their host was invariably making biscuits. Anyway, the food was always worth the wait.

"During the first rush of nouvelle cuisine," Gross wrote, Bailey served chicken pot pie and "the best boiled beef I've ever eaten." Even the lowliest vegetables were transformed in his hands. To this day, two of my favorite side dishes are his shredded, buttered cabbage and grated turnips braised in chicken stock. The steamed okra in a tomato vinaigrette that I served at one of my first full-fledged, grown-up dinner parties met, much to my relief, with huge success.

Both Bailey and Cantwell grew up in small towns—the former in Bunkie, Louisiana (population 5,000), and the latter in Bristol, Rhode Island—among family they clearly loved, two facts that explain, I think, their warm and relaxed approach to entertaining. In an especially funny article, Cantwell wrote about how often, in the course of particularly trying domestic duties, she asked herself if the Queen of England—"the pole star against which I measure my life"—would have to go through what she did. She described trying to type in an apartment that had no heat and carrying a chair by herself for blocks to be repaired. In the end, though, she realized that she had the one thing "the Queen of England cannot have, and that is my secure conviction that my friends like me for myself alone." She may have been unable to offer guests a warm room or cloth napkins while living in a temporary apartment. "Still," she wrote, "they show up to dine."

She knew, as Bailey did, that celebrations were not necessarily about pomp, that it is silly to postpone pleasure for an event—or an apartment—worthy of it. In *City Food*, Bailey has a whole chapter on "Celebration Dinners," and in its introduction he lists reasons to give them, ranging from a pay raise to a friend's birthday. The recipe for angel hair pasta is from a menu with the apt title "A Simple Swell Dinner," and it is perfect for an intimate New Year's Eve. So is Cantwell's Steak in Champagne, an elegant and supremely easy concoction inspired by her theory that Champagne should never lie dormant in the refrigerator waiting for a special occasion that may never arise. In the text that accompanies the recipe, she quotes Macheath's haunting line from *The Threepenny Opera*—"in real life the messenger never comes"—and reminds her readers that "one has to be one's own messenger." She and Bailey taught us well how to do that.

LEE BAILEY'S PASTA WITH GOLDEN CAVIAR

YIELD: 8 SERVINGS

. . .

3 cups crème fraîche

⅓ cup Calvados or other brandy

2 bay leaves

8 tablespoons (1 stick) unsalted butter, softened

1½ pounds angel hair pasta

1 egg yolk

20 ounces golden (whitefish) caviar

Salt

Freshly ground black pepper

Combine the crème fraîche, Calvados, and bay leaves in a large saucepan and whisk until blended. Heat to boiling over medium heat. Reduce the heat to very low and keep warm, stirring occasionally while cooking the pasta.

Meanwhile, bring a large pot of salted water to a boil. Add 3 tablespoons of the butter and all of the pasta. Cook until the pasta is just done, still firm to the teeth, 3 to 4 minutes. Drain and keep warm.

Whisk the egg yolk and the remaining 5 tablespoons of butter in a large serving bowl until blended. Add the hot pasta and toss gently to coat the strands. Discard the bay leaves and pour the crème-fraîche mixture over the pasta. Add about three-fourths of the caviar and toss gently until mixed. Season to taste with salt and freshly ground black pepper. Serve at once on warm plates, topping each with a heaping spoonful of the remaining caviar.

NOTE: Golden caviar is available with 24-hour notice from Wild Edibles, in the Market at Grand Central Terminal, (212) 687-4255.

MARY CANTWELL'S STEAK IN CHAMPAGNE

YIELD: 2 SERVINGS

. . .

2 tablespoons plus 1 teaspoon butter

1 teaspoon olive oil

2 filet mignons, at least 6 ounces each

Salt

2 shallots, minced

½ cup brut champagne

Freshly ground black pepper

Cut the 2 tablespoons of butter into small pieces and set aside.

Melt the remaining 1 teaspoon of butter in the olive oil in a small skillet. Turn the heat to high and sear the steaks on both sides. Lower the heat and cook to desired doneness, about 4 minutes total on each side for medium-rare.

Remove the steaks to a heated platter and sprinkle with salt. Add the shallots to the skillet and sauté for 1 minute. Add the champagne and boil over high heat to reduce quickly by two-thirds.

Remove the pan from the heat and swirl in the butter pieces and a few grains of freshly ground black pepper. Pour the sauce over the steaks and serve.

LEMONADE SOUFFLÉ

Butter for greasing the dish

5 eggs, separated

¼ cup granulated sugar

5 tablespoons frozen lemonade concentrate, thawed

Pinch of salt

Confectioners' sugar for dusting

Preheat the oven to 350 degrees. Butter an 8-cup soufflé dish. Beat the egg yolks and sugar until pale yellow. Stir in the lemonade concentrate. Set aside.

Using clean beaters, beat the egg whites with the salt until soft peaks form. Fold one-third of the whites into the yolk mixture; then gently fold in the rest, being careful not to deflate the mixture. Turn into the prepared dish.

Bake on the center rack for 20 to 25 minutes, until the top is a rich, golden brown. Dust with confectioners' sugar and serve immediately.

Into Plein-Air

❖

In his introduction to *Ten Vineyard Lunches*, Richard Olney writes that every meal, even the daily ones spent "for the most part in solitude," is "a celebration." But, he adds, "the most wonderful are those of the summer months . . . At the dinner hour, the terrace, laced with colored lights, is transformed into a funny little theater with a vaguely carnival atmosphere."

My terrace does not at the moment have colored lights, but I know exactly what Olney means. It is somehow more festive to dine out in the open, but there is an ease about it, too. Olney, who lived in Provence until his death in 1999, wrote that in planning outdoor meals, his menus seemed to come together effortlessly—most of the ingredients, after all, were taken from the garden, and skewers of lamb or scallops could be finished quickly on the grill. Wines from his adopted home, especially the excellent Bandols from Domaine Tempier, suddenly seemed to go perfectly with everything on his warm-weather table.

Something simple and salady almost always began Olney's midday meal—sliced tomatoes and onions topped with torn basil and drizzled with olive oil and herb vinegar, or parboiled vegetables tossed in vinaigrette. At the end of the instructions for his favorite tossed salad, a colorful preparation adorned with nasturtium blossoms, he writes, "I know of nothing more beautiful than the out-of-doors summer light playing across its surface."

I don't know if Olney was also a painter, but he sure sounds like one, and the salads he made were a lot like those enjoyed a century earlier by Monet at Giverny. Monet was not a cook, but he loved to dine well, to lunch in his gorgeous walled garden (which in summer boasted a profusion of nasturtiums) or to picnic a little farther afield.

In his painting *Luncheon on the Grass* (1865–66), the cloth on the ground is covered with pâtés and grapes and what looks like one of the roasted game birds he was partial to. In *Luncheon* (1873), the meal is over, and all that is left on the outdoor table is a silver coffeepot and a bowl of peaches, along with some bread and a bit of red wine in a glass.

Like Olney and his salad, Monet was obsessed with light, and it influenced his meals, but in a different way—lunch was always at 11:30 sharp so that it would be over in time for him to take advantage of the afternoon sun. He rarely allowed his guests, who ranged from Pissarro and Renoir to the statesman Georges Clemenceau, to arrive on their own, preferring to send for them so that they wouldn't be late.

Once they got there, they were lucky. According to *Monet's Table: The Cooking Journals of Claude Monet*, they dined on pike from his pond, along with vegetables, fruit, and even mushrooms from his garden. He served salads of dandelion leaves and strips of bacon, or chicory with garlic and croutons. (He favored so much salt and pepper on the salad that no one else could eat it, so there were always two bowls on the table.) He grew sweet peppers and chili peppers, lima beans and green beans, zucchini, and red and yellow tomatoes. (Olney, who writes that he "can ill support a day without a tomato salad at one meal or the other," would have approved.)

Some of Monet's illustrious guests sang for their supper. He got his recipe for bouillabaisse from Cezanne and one for bread rolls from Millet. Rodin once sent over Isadora Duncan, who, naturally, danced.

Monet favored cakes for dessert, and on special occasions ice cream was made in a hand-cranked tub and frozen in a conical mold. Olney's desserts, especially in the evenings, when they usually followed cheese, were lighter fare. My favorite is a simple gratin of fresh figs (figs halved and drizzled with Chartreuse and honey, dabbed with crème fraîche, and run under a broiler until bubbling) served with a glass of Muscat de Beaumes-de-Venise.

I am sick that I never dined on Olney's terrace, and I wish I could crawl into one of Monet's luncheon paintings, but when the weather is right I happily make do in my own garden where the vine-covered pergola provides shade above my long French metal table.

Monet and Olney were both partial to Champagne as an aperitif, and in the summer, I especially agree. Monet liked Veuve Clicquot; I like Billecart-Salmon rosé because it tastes so good and looks so pretty.

One of my outdoor standbys is a tomatoey crab soup served from a tureen at the table. It is based on a recipe from *The Picayune Creole Cookbook*, first published in 1901 and made infinitely easier by the availability of fresh lump crabmeat already out of the shell. The original recipe was flavored with parsley, "sweet marjoram," and thyme.

Damon Lee Fowler, the food historian and cookbook author, adds mint to his version, pointing out that early Southern settlers used it often, and it is an unexpected and wonderful addition. I throw in tarragon, too, and serve the soup with biscuits split and buttered, sandwiched with a slice of Smithfield ham. French bread would be fine, of course, but cured ham and crabmeat go way back, both being plentiful and popular items along the Southeastern seaboard. (Crab Norfolk is a classic sauté of crabmeat and to me is best with slivers of country ham.)

Sometimes, I precede the soup with one of Olney's salads or haricots verts tossed in oil and vinegar, and at lunch I might follow with pound cake. Surprisingly, the recipe I use, and which I think of as a staple of old-fashioned Southern cuisine, is almost identical to the pound cake in *Monet's Table*. (There is also a recipe for fish Creole, a fish sauced with butter, tomatoes, cayenne pepper, lemon, and herbs—the same ingredients as in the crab soup.)

At dinner, I follow it up with homemade ice cream. Among my favorite recipes are those from Justine's restaurant in Memphis, which, in its day, was famous for its crabmeat, homemade ice cream, and spectacular rose garden.

At parties, Justine would pile both her lotus and her mint ice cream in silver punch bowls and serve them from the sideboard. I can think of nothing grander and more delicious than ice cream served instead on a table under the stars, especially when accompanied by a porcelain platter of thin toasted slices of the leftover pound cake.

CREOLE CRAB SOUP

YIELD: 4 TO 6 SERVINGS

. . .

2 large lemons

3 tablespoons butter

1 medium yellow onion,
    peeled and chopped

2 garlic cloves, minced

4 cups canned peeled
    Italian tomatoes, seeded
    and chopped, with their
    juice

4 cups shellfish stock or fish
    stock

1 bay leaf

1 large sprig flat-leaf parsley

1 sprig fresh marjoram

1 tablespoon chopped fresh
    mint, plus 1 tablespoon
    for serving

1 tablespoon chopped fresh
    tarragon

1 pound lump crabmeat

Salt

Pinch of cayenne pepper

Using a vegetable peeler, remove the zest from 1 lemon in one long strip, if possible; set aside. Juice the peeled lemon. Thinly slice the remaining lemon into 4 to 6 pieces; set aside for garnish.

Melt the butter in a deep, large skillet or Dutch oven over medium heat and sauté the onion and garlic until soft, about 4 minutes. Add the tomatoes with their juice and the stock, and turn the heat up to medium-high. When the mixture boils, lower to a simmer. Add the bay leaf and the rest of the herbs, the lemon zest strip, and 1½ tablespoons of the lemon juice. Simmer, partly covered, for 30 to 45 minutes.

Add the crabmeat and simmer gently until the soup is slightly thickened, about 10 minutes. Add the salt, cayenne, and more lemon juice to taste. Discard the bay leaf, parsley, and marjoram sprigs. Add the remaining tablespoon of fresh mint at the last minute. Spoon the soup into bowls, and top each serving with a lemon slice.

JUSTINE'S PINEAPPLE MINT ICE CREAM

. . .

1½ cups sugar

2 cups fresh mint leaves, lightly packed

½ cup light corn syrup

2 cups canned crushed pineapple in its own juice

1½ cups pineapple juice

2 cups milk

2 cups heavy cream

½ cup white crème de menthe

¼ cup freshly squeezed lemon juice

In a medium saucepan, combine the sugar with 1½ cups water, bring to a boil over medium-high heat, and cook until the sugar dissolves. Continue to boil, without stirring, for about 10 minutes, or until it reaches the soft-ball stage (234 to 240 degrees on a candy thermometer), or when a drop forms a soft ball in a cup of cold water. Stir in the mint and simmer over medium heat 10 minutes more. Remove from heat and let cool.

Pour the mint syrup into a blender and puree; then strain into a large mixing bowl. Stir in the corn syrup. Puree the pineapple and pineapple juice in a blender and add it to the mint-syrup mixture, along with the milk, cream, crème de menthe, and lemon juice. Chill at least 4 hours, or overnight, and freeze in an ice-cream machine according to the manufacturer's directions.

MARTHA PEARL VILLAS'S
POUND CAKE

YIELD: 12 SERVINGS

* * *

1 pound (4 sticks) butter

1 pound (2 cups) sugar

9 large eggs

1 pound (4 cups) all-purpose flour

Dash of salt

2 teaspoons vanilla extract

Juice of 1 lemon

Preheat the oven to 325 degrees. Grease and flour a 10-inch tube or Bundt pan.

In a large bowl, cream the butter with an electric mixer, then gradually add the sugar, continuing to beat until well creamed and smooth. Add the eggs one at a time, beating well after each addition. Gradually add the flour and salt, beating constantly. Add the extract and lemon juice and continue beating until well blended.

Pour the batter into the prepared pan and "spank" the bottom of the pan to distribute the batter evenly. Bake until a straw inserted into the cake comes out clean, about 1 hour 15 minutes, taking care not to over bake. Let the cake cool in the pan for 5 minutes. Turn the cake out onto a rack and let cool.

Tip of the Iceberg

❖

In the thirty years since the dawn of "American Regional Cooking"—a movement recently and entertainingly documented by one of its founders Jeremiah Tower, in *California Dish: What I Saw (and Cooked) at the American Culinary Revolution*—iceberg lettuce has been flat-out maligned in some quarters and simply ignored in others. When Alice Waters served her first salad of "baby greens" at Chez Panisse, it was truly revolutionary; now it's *de rigueur*. Just about every supermarket chain in America sells prewashed bags of mesclun, along with herb mix, Asian mix, baby spinach, and baby romaine. The watershed moment for me came sometime in the late 1990s, when I sat down to dinner at Jack Binion's restaurant in the Horseshoe Casino in Tunica, Mississippi, and there on the menu were the words "mesclun salad."

My jaw almost hit the table. First, there was a tiny amount of pride over the fact that my home state had finally discovered field greens. Then there was the realization that the so-called revolution or "California Cuisine" or the "New American Cooking" was no longer a trend but The Way We Eat Now. But there was also a serious pang of disappointment. I had been hankering for a bowl of torn up iceberg tossed in some Thousand Island dressing. And if I couldn't get that in a casino just off Highway 61 about a half-hour south of Memphis, Tennessee, where was a girl to go?

Fortunately, now that we have entered the twenty-first century, and "new" American cooking has incorporated some of our older traditions, iceberg is making something of a comeback. Robert Carter, the chef at one of my favorite American restaurants, the Peninsula Grill, in Charleston, South Carolina, features an ice-cold wedge topped with delicious buttermilk dressing and sprinkled with equally delicious bacon "jerky" (bacon that has been slowly rendered, rather than fried quickly), and I am not the only customer who orders it repeatedly. "People love it," Carter says. "People you'd never expect to like it like it. Not just the rednecks like me." Indeed, the most popular salad on the menu at the coffee shop at the Beverly Hills Hotel is Gary's Salad, composed of chopped iceberg, turkey, egg whites, onion, oil and vinegar, and Russian dressing—but then, of course, L.A. never went as mesclun crazy as its neighbor to the north. The hotel's Polo Lounge offers another popular salad, the McCarthy (named after a regular guest, not Kevin or Eugene or, God forbid, Joe), made of iceberg and romaine, along with chopped chicken, hard-boiled eggs, cheddar, bacon, beets, and tomatoes.

Maybe the denizens of Beverly Hills like iceberg because its high water content makes them feel skinny. Carter, who does have "wild corn lettuce" on his menu (alongside grilled sea scallops and cheddar corn fritters), says he finds iceberg more "soothing and refreshing." And, he says, "When it's really cold, the water inside the leaves is almost frozen." The fact that the leaves are also virtually tasteless is a plus. Iceberg is all about texture—it's the perfect delivery system for rich dressings like Thousand Island and blue cheese and Carter's buttermilk, though he took a risk when he first offered up his salad. A local critic had recently panned another restaurant whose crime had been to serve iceberg. "I put mine on knowing that," Carter says, "but it was such a big hit, now several upscale restaurants in town have it on the menu."

You can sort of see where the critic was coming from. The iceberg salads of my youth were rarely as elegant as Carter's combination of chilled plate and well-dressed wedge. More often, you were given those thin plastic "wooden" bowls full of listless lettuce, wilted at the edges, topped with shredded carrots already gone chalky, and "bacon bits" that weren't made of bacon. The dressings came in a carousel: gelatinous "Italian," Day-Glo orange "French," pink, pickle-flecked Thousand Island that sat out so long it usually had a slightly darker pink crust on the top. Still, it was the Thousand Island—and the ubiquitous basket of cellophane-wrapped saltines—that usually saved the day. Somehow it seemed to have fewer sugars and dyes in it, and its roots were a tad more refined. According to Craig Claiborne, it may have been invented at Chicago's Drake Hotel by a chef who had recently visited the Thousand Islands in upstate New York with his wife. When she viewed his new creation, with all its chopped up chunks of goodies, she told him that it reminded her of the sea of little islands they'd just seen.

Thousand Island that you've made yourself poured over a wedge or some crispy torn iceberg is a wonderful thing. So is my friend Gary Smith's incredible blue-cheese dressing tossed with iceberg and sliced onion and radishes, but he won't give me the recipe. However, my very favorite new iceberg salad is found in *The Gift of Southern Cooking* by Edna Lewis and Scott Peacock. With the "BLT Salad," the duo has achieved the impossible—they've created something even more perfect than a BLT. The salad is the sandwich in a bowl: a head of iceberg, about eight slices of toasted white bread, 10 or 12 slices of crispy bacon, and four tomatoes, all cut into one-inch pieces and tossed with mayonnaise, salt, and lots of freshly ground black pepper. The toast and the bacon should still be warm, the tomatoes should be really ripe, and the mayo should be homemade with a whisk so that it is loose enough to work.

I also adore torn iceberg lettuce tossed in a garlic-rubbed wooden bowl with tomatoes, sliced onion, lemon juice, oil, and salt and pepper. This is the salad I have eaten all my life at the incomparable Doe's Eat Place in Greenville, Mississippi. The bowl at Doe's, with its decades of seasoning, is the secret of its salad, along with Aunt Florence Signa and Little Doe's wife "Sug," whose hands do something amazing to the mix. People bring in their wooden bowls and leave them at the restaurant for a year or two, in hopes that the ladies will toss enough of their salads in them that they'll soak up some of the magic. A variation on this salad is also found about seven miles away at Lillo's in Leland, Mississippi, where it is billed as an "Italian salad," and where it also includes chopped up green olives and anchovies.

I went to school with Charles Lillo, the third-generation proprietor, and I really like his salad (and his excellent thin-crust pizzas and the catfish Parmesan with tomato sauce), but the real reason I love Lillo's is that it is the site of one of my father's better lines. A friend of my parents had recently divorced and was dating a younger woman, a former beauty queen, who did not have a lot to say when they came to my parents' house for drinks before going out to Lillo's. (In those days it was called Lillo's Dine and Dance.) When they pulled up, they could hear the music from the jukebox spilling out into the parking lot, and as soon as the beauty queen got out of the car, she started gyrating and carrying on. The transformation was, apparently, remarkable, and prompted my father to look at my mother and say, "She ain't much in a parlor, but she's hell in a tonk."

Now, that story does not have all that much to do with salad, but it does have to do with the days when you could go out and have a cocktail and a cigarette and a turn or two around a dance floor before sitting down to some food that was actually pretty good. We lost something when we got too embarrassed to celebrate the food we grew up eating, when food became so overwrought that, in the words of my friend Will Feltus, restaurants needed "spell-check on their computers just to print the menus." The pendulum has swung back a bit now. And chefs like Robert Carter offer not just good ol' iceberg, but also shrimp cocktail and steak *au poivre* and lamb chops with bearnaise sauce, not to mention the best coconut cake I have ever put in my mouth (thankfully available at www.peninsulagrill. com). "My philosophy is to serve the food great," says Carter. "I tell my sous-chefs, 'Poach the damn shrimp correctly and cook the *au poivre* correctly and you'll be famous.'" What a refreshing philosophy—as refreshing as his ice-cold iceberg-lettuce salad.

ICEBERG WITH SMOKED-BACON-AND-BUTTERMILK DRESSING

(Adapted from Robert Carter, Peninsula Grill)

YIELD: 8 SERVINGS

* * *

2 heads iceberg lettuce

8 ripe Roma tomatoes, sliced thin

2 cups buttermilk herb dressing (recipe to follow)

12 slices smoked bacon, diced into ½-inch pieces (about 2
cups), and fried

Trim the loose outer leaves from the heads of iceberg, cut each into 4 wedges, and place in the freezer for 10 minutes before serving, along with 4 serving plates.

Remove the chilled plates and arrange each with a circle of sliced tomatoes. Set a wedge in the center of each plate. Nap with ¼ cup of the dressing.

Sprinkle bacon over each wedge. Serve immediately.

BUTTERMILK HERB DRESSING

YIELD: ABOUT 3 CUPS

· · ·

1½ cups sour cream

1 cup buttermilk

½ cup Hellmann's mayonnaise

½ cup grated Asiago or Parmesan cheese

2 tablespoons chopped fresh basil

2 tablespoons chopped fresh chives

4 teaspoons finely chopped fresh parsley

4 teaspoons cider vinegar

2 teaspoons sugar

2 teaspoons minced garlic

2 teaspoons Worcestershire sauce

1 healthy pinch of salt

1 healthy pinch of freshly ground white pepper

Combine all ingredients in a bowl and mix well. Chill overnight to allow flavors to develop.

THOUSAND ISLAND DRESSING

YIELD: ABOUT 2 CUPS

, , ,

1 hard-boiled egg, chopped

1 cup homemade or Hellmann's mayonnaise

¼ cup chili sauce or ketchup

2 tablespoons finely chopped pimento-stuffed green olives

1 to 2 tablespoons finely chopped sweet pickle

1 tablespoon chopped onion

2 teaspoons finely chopped fresh parsley

½ to 1 teaspoon fresh lemon juice

Salt and freshly ground pepper to taste

Combine the egg, mayonnaise, chili sauce, olives, 1 tablespoon pickle, the onion, parsley, and ½ teaspoon lemon juice in a mixing bowl and blend well. Taste and season with salt and pepper. Add more chopped pickle and lemon juice as desired.

Swan Song

❊

When I found out that La Côte Basque was closing its doors, I was sad—irrationally so, since it later occurred to me that I hadn't actually eaten there in almost fourteen years. I remember the occasion clearly because it was the birthday of my ex-fiancé, almost a year to the date that I had sort of, more or less, left him at the altar. Still guilt-ridden (but happily about to leave New York for an extended stay in New Orleans), I thought I should create a celebration, one in which we'd emphasize his birthday rather than my departure and finally close the door on what was left of our relationship. So I assembled my own version of Truman Capote's swans, those chic society ladies like Babe Paley and Gloria Guinness; mine were Joan Buck, Kathleen Tynan, and my childhood friend M.T., and they did not let me down. We hauled out all our jewels and finery (I wore a black Chanel suit, my first), picked up the birthday boy in a Town Car, and spent the rest of the night lavishly fussing over him—and drinking, a lot. We started with champagne and caviar and the excellent foie gras terrine and progressed through many bottles of Puligny-Montrachet to those chocolate and Grand Marnier soufflés you had to order ahead of time. When the bill arrived, I didn't flinch—the entire evening had been a triumph of sophisticated merriment.

Looking back on it, the entire evening, or at least the thinking behind it, seems more like a triumph of insanity. I had obviously lost my mind. But somehow the restaurant itself made the occasion less bizarre, okay even, with all the cosseting and the red banquettes, the completely charming captains with their occasional raised eyebrows and knowing almost-smiles, the perfect choreography of waiters and busboys and sommeliers that made you feel as if they existed only to do your bidding even though the room was, thankfully, packed. It was possible not to know what year it was or even what city. We were there to indulge and be jolly, and we somehow succeeded at both.

I first learned about La Côte Basque, like a lot of people, from Capote's infamous short story, published in *Esquire* in 1975. I knew who all the characters were (I was a devout reader of my mother's *Vogues* and *Women's Wear Dailys*), and I loved having this thrillingly revealing window into all these supposedly glamorous lives. The news that one of Capote's victims, Ann Woodward (Ann Hopkins in the story), killed herself just before it hit the stands made it all the way down to the Mississippi Delta.

Upon the demise of its namesake, I reread "La Côte Basque" and found it not thrilling but poisonous and more than a little boring. If I'd been any of those thinly disguised women, I wouldn't have killed myself, I'd have killed Capote. But then he didn't exactly survive it. The best parts involved the legendarily haughty Henri Soulé fussing because Lady Coolbirth was drinking too much (he "disapproved of customers dulling their taste buds with alcohol"), and because the soufflé Furstenberg she ordered, "a froth of cheese and spinach into which an assortment of poached eggs has been sunk strategically," was such a "nuisance," indeed, "an uproar." There are very few places left where the kitchens produce what can properly be called uproars, those complicated Escoffier recipes that require hours of prep work and involve multiple sauces and compound butters and garnitures. Soulé, who also owned the even more legendary Le Pavillon, has been dead since 1966. (He died in the bathroom at La Côte Basque and the restaurant passed into the hands of his longtime mistress, a former hatcheck girl named Henriette Spalter), and soufflé Furstenburg hasn't been on the menu in years. But Jean-Jacques Rachou, who bought La Côte Basque from Madame Henriette, kept most everything else— lobster bisque, sautéed sweetbreads Barigoule, filet of sole with mustard sauce, quenelles de brochet with sauce Nantua—as well as the splashy murals of the French seacoast.

Rachou knew what he was doing; under his tutelage, Charlie Palmer, Todd English, Rick Moonen, and Waldy Malouf became great chefs in their own right. I got to know his cooking well; for a period in the mid-1980s I was something of a regular. And not just at misguided birthday parties, but at lunch, accompanied by big shots who had by then replaced the ladies at the coveted banquettes. I was overseeing a special issue of *U.S. News & World Report* called "The New American Establishment," and since this new establishment was much like the old, La Côte Basque was where they dined, usually on poached salmon right off the cart, in the interest of time. After a memorable meal with the leveraged-buyout king Teddy Forstmann, he asked me back to his office to meet an Afghan rebel general, a "freedom fighter" against the Soviets whom Forstmann was financing (a philanthropic gesture that apparently suited him better than donating a wing to the Met). Ted's wonderful late brother Nicky was there, and then we met the rebel, a short, fat man in fatigues who was extremely pleased with himself, especially after Ted wrote him the check, which, if I recall correctly, was for well over a million dollars.

Anyway, those days are long gone in more ways than one, and my last trip to La Côte Basque, two nights before it closed in March of 2004, was a little sad. The place seemed too bright somehow; and the flowers were garish mums and anthuriums; and on the tables there were bud vases of some unidentifiable foliage instead of the yellow roses whose petals Carol Matthau crushed between her fingers in Capote's story. I hadn't seen so much curly parsley since my grandmother died, but the terrine of foie gras was as delicious as ever and the housemade pâtés still first-rate. I was afraid that the quenelles would not be, so I didn't order them, and now I may never be able to again.

And yet, Julia Child has an exhaustive lesson on how to make quenelles in Volume One of *Mastering the Art of French Cooking*, which, as she points out, are startlingly easy to make now that the food processor exists. There's also a recipe for sauce Nantua, a sinfully good cream-and-egg-yolk fish sauce that is enriched with shellfish butter and has a garniture of crawfish tails. (It is excellent on almost any poached fish, and the good news is that shelled crawfish tails are now sold in one-pound bags.) So I have started making these classics myself, along with other forgotten treasures like *pots de crème*, the dessert I had on my first visit at fourteen to La Grenouille, which is thankfully still with us. Lutèce has also shut its doors permanently as has La Caravelle, but Rachou has reopened La Côte Basque as a brasserie. He's smart—the era's over. But we can re-create it occasionally in our dining rooms. A good way to begin is with this easy but elegant oyster velouté from Paula Wolfert's *The Cooking of South-West France* (the real *Côte Basque*). And my friend Jeremiah Tower has promised to make me crab quenelles the next time he's in my kitchen. When he does, I shall do my part and make like a swan, dressed to the nines and ready to be indulged.

OYSTER VELOUTÉ
WITH BLACK CAVIAR

Adapted from Paula Wolfert's The Cooking of South-West France

YIELD: 6 TO 8 SERVINGS

* * *

3 tablespoons unsalted
   butter

2 shallots, finely chopped

3 tablespoons all-purpose
   flour

3 cups unsalted fish stock

3 cups unsalted chicken
   stock

⅓ teaspoon sea salt

1½ cups shucked oysters,
   including their liquor

Pinch of cayenne pepper

3 large egg yolks

1 cup heavy cream

Few drops fresh lemon juice

3 tablespoons black caviar

In a saucepan, melt the butter and soften the shallots in the butter but do not brown. Blend in the flour and cook over low heat, stirring often, for 10 minutes. (The roux should be smooth and golden.) In another saucepan, combine and warm the stocks. Gradually add the stocks to the roux, stirring constantly, and bring to a boil. Reduce the heat and simmer for 20 minutes, skimming off any scum that forms on the top. Add salt to taste.

Strain the oysters and reserve their liquor. Puree the oysters in a food processor or blender and add them with their liquor to the soup. Simmer, partly covered, for 5 minutes, then add the cayenne. Strain the soup through a fine sieve, pressing hard with a spoon. (The soup may be prepared ahead to this point.)

About 5 or 10 minutes before serving, reheat the soup. Whisk the egg yolks and cream together. Slowly whisk in a cup of the hot soup, then stir the cream mixture back into the soup. Stir constantly over low heat, until the soup thickens slightly. Bring *almost* at a boil and remove from the heat. Add the lemon juice and taste and adjust the seasonings. Ladle the velouté into serving bowls and top each serving with about a teaspoon of caviar.

NOTE: To serve cold, chill the soup over ice, then refrigerate. When ready to serve, thin with a bit of half-and-half.

LEMON CARAMEL POTS DE CRÉME

Adapted from Luscious Lemon Desserts, *by Lori Longbotham*

YIELD: 6 SERVINGS

＊ ＊ ＊

1½ cups heavy cream

¼ cup finely grated lemon zest (from 2 to 3 lemons)

1 teaspoon whole coriander seeds

¾ cup sugar

6 large egg yolks

¼ cup fresh lemon juice

Pinch of salt

Position a rack in the middle of the oven and preheat the oven to 325 degrees. Have ready six ½-cup *pots-de-crème* cups or ramekins and a baking pan large enough to hold them.

In a saucepan, bring the cream, zest, and coriander seeds just to a boil. Remove from heat, cover, and let stand for 10 minutes.

In a heavy saucepan, heat the sugar and a ¼ cup water over medium heat, stirring, until the sugar dissolves. Increase the heat to high and boil, without stirring, until the mixture becomes deep amber, occasionally brushing down the sides of the pan with a wet pastry brush and swirling the pan. Carefully whisk in the cream combination. (The mixture will sputter, so be careful.) Reduce the heat to low and cook, stirring, until the caramel dissolves. Remove the pan from heat.

Gently whisk together the egg yolks, lemon juice, and salt. Very slowly whisk in the hot cream mixture. Strain through a fine sieve or a sieve lined with layers of cheesecloth. Let stand about 3 minutes, then spoon off any foam.

Divide the custard among the cups or ramekins, cover with aluminum foil (put lids on the cups), and place them in the baking pan. Add enough hot tap water to come halfway up the sides of the molds. Bake until the custards are just set around the edges but trembling in the centers, 40 to 45 minutes.

Remove ramekins from the oven and from the pan. Let cool and refrigerate, loosely covered, for at least 3 hours and up to 24. Serve without unmolding.

The Comeback Kid

I owe my much-valued friendship with the screenwriter Robert Harling to the brilliant American chef Jeremiah Tower and his intrepid imagination. Years ago, Bobby and I were seated next to each other at a dinner party in New Orleans, and somehow (though not, sadly, because it was what we were being served) we got onto the subject of Château d'Yquem. I knew, vaguely, that Bobby had written some movies (and later I learned that he had written some of my favorites, including *Steel Magnolias* and *Soapdish*), and I knew he had a big old plantation house in Natchitoches, Louisiana, and I knew he was friends with our hostess, who was a good friend of mine. But none of that impressed me nearly as much as the fact that he had read the same tiny aside I had in Tower's first book, *Jeremiah Tower's New American Classics*, on the merits—and the decadence—of drinking Château d'Yquem with a "rich, aged, perfectly cooked roast beef."

Now Bobby and I both knew all about the merits of drinking this most extravagant of all sauternes with ripe nectarines or juicy mangoes or a fine terrine of foie gras. We knew it often married well with shellfish, especially lobster, and we certainly knew that it was damn good on its own. But I had puzzled over Tower's audacious combination for years, and I was delighted to find that someone else had, too, and even more delighted when he proposed that we try it at his house, with him cooking and providing the wine. So we did, carefully following the instructions about "chewing the beef and taking a draft of the wine, chewing twice and swallowing," and it was every bit as "rapturous" and life-changing as Tower promised it would be. That meal not only cemented my friendship with Bobby, it also upheld my conviction that Tower is a genius.

By then Tower had already changed the landscape of American cuisine as part owner and head chef at Chez Panisse in Berkeley. He had also created Stars in San Francisco, one of the world's great restaurants, a fabulous, improbably intimate "grand café" in the style of La Coupole in Paris when it was still cool, but with incredible, then-new food, like salmon tartare and grilled duck with mango-chili salsa, Tower's famous black-bean cake and tiny, perfect pizzas at the bar. I loved Stars, and I used *New American Classics* like a bible, but even before that, I was saved from poverty by Time-Life's "Good Cook" series, for which Tower served as consultant under the great Richard Olney.

This was well over twenty-five years ago, when I was living in Washington and taking as many semesters off from college as I attended. Fed up with this pattern, my parents ceased to be what I would describe as supportive, so I augmented my meager wages at *Newsweek,* where I worked in the afternoons, with a morning job sitting in a cubicle and selling those "Good Cook" books over the phone. I was only twenty, but I knew they were something special—with their historical references and brilliantly curated recipes from all over the world and their clear photos that served as foolproof step-by-step guides through endless dishes and techniques (photos that, I later found out, had been Tower's doing). Genuinely inspired, I sold so many of them that I won the whole series as a prize, and more important, I could actually afford to go grocery shopping. By the time I finally got a degree, I had very little recollection of what I had learned in class, but I possessed an impressive repertoire of dishes that I could make entirely from the memory of the pictures in those volumes, called simply *Poultry* or *Pasta* or *Desserts*.

When Tower sold Stars in San Francisco and went off to the Far East to open a version of it there, I thought the memory of that momentous dinner with Bobby, my stained copy of Jeremiah Tower's *New American Classics* (now out of print), and the Time-Life photographs of Tower's hands leading me through fabulous variations on, say, a simple salad of poached chicken slices arrayed on a glistening tomato vinaigrette were all that I would have left of my hero. But then, thankfully, he came back with *Jeremiah Tower Cooks*, a collection of 250 recipes, charming anecdotes about his well-traveled life, and invaluable insights for the home cook, ranging from why you should never plunge vegetables into an ice bath ("You might as well save yourself the time and trouble and buy frozen ones instead") to what is wrong with all those "sprigs of fresh herbs sticking out of the top of every dish today" ("Let's decide that garnishes . . . should be edible and an integral part of the dish").

Tower is refreshingly straightforward, but he has definitely retained his decadent side. In the new book, there's an oyster soup that takes only fifteen minutes to make, but its key ingredient is osetra caviar, and a sea urchin soufflé Tower once baked, in its own shell, for James Beard, who pronounced it the best thing he ever tasted. There's a section on sandwiches that begins modestly enough with a chicken club and an open-faced egg salad, but the one I intend to try first is the open-faced foie gras on toasted brioche, topped with a tangle of arugula leaves tossed with chopped preserved lemon, hazelnut oil, and cardamom. There are directions for making the perfect hamburger and a list of toppings, including a simple one of sour cream mixed with coarsely ground black pepper. But on the next page there's a recipe for a truffled burger that he recommends having with "a luscious, old-fashioned, rich and powerful red wine—in a large balloon glass," lest the burger "falls short of its overwhelming effect."

These days, thanks to Daniel Boulud's delicious version at DB Bistro (which also contains foie gras and minced short ribs), burgers with black truffles are all the rage. But Tower first wrote about them, for me, when I was an assigning editor at *Vogue* in December 1988. (I remember being so happy when I read the first line of that article—"Christmas seems so obvious"—because I knew something good was going to follow, and it did.)

Tower can really write, and it is not surprising, since he counts among his influences the wonderful English food writer Elizabeth David. But he was also inspired by Escoffier and Olney and Beard, and by his colorful Russian aunt and uncle who taught him the pleasures of everything from a rustic coleslaw to caviar and blini. The result is a cuisine I call sensuous simplicity. Also, even though Tower is nothing if not modern, he knows that there are not, in fact, all that many ways to skin a cat, that it is still way worth knowing how to make a flawless hollandaise sauce, a mousse-like, green-goddess mayonnaise, and a real Russian dressing with horseradish and caviar.

One of my favorite recipes in the whole book is for Montpelier butter—it's the best version I've ever tried and incredibly versatile. In *New American Classics*, Tower wrote that this classic compound butter "transforms hot cauliflower" and that "on top of mashed potatoes it is so good that it should be arrested." Here he says he hasn't changed his mind and further recommends it with hot grilled fish or steaks and, at room temperature, with cold poached salmon. With typical passion, he adds that when it is spooned between slices of leftover roast pork or veal "with the slices reassembled, left for a day, and then eaten at cool room temperature, it creates a lifelong memory." I guess that will be Bobby's and my next project.

"BURNT" PASSION-FRUIT CURD

Adapted from Jeremiah Tower Cooks

YIELD: 4 SERVINGS

∘ ∘ ∘

4 eggs

2 egg yolks

1 cup fresh passion-fruit
juice (from about 6
large ripe fruits, pulp
removed, pureed in a
blender for 1 minute
and sieved; see Note)

2 tablespoons fresh lime
juice

¼ cup heavy cream

1 cup granulated sugar

Pinch of salt

½ cup unsalted butter, at
room temperature, cut
into tablespoon-size
pieces

¼ cup superfine sugar

Combine all the ingredients except the butter and superfine sugar in a metal nonreactive bowl and beat together until the 1 cup of sugar is completely dissolved. Prepare an ice bath in a bowl slightly bigger than the bowl used to beat the ingredients. Put the bowl with the egg mixture over simmering water and cook, beating constantly, for 10 minutes, or until the curd thickens, being careful not to let the egg mixture curdle. Beat in the butter. Transfer the bowl to the ice bath and beat the curd until it is cold, about 5 minutes.

Spoon the curd into four cold, shallow gratin dishes. Cover and refrigerate for at least 2 hours.

When ready to serve, heat the broiler to maximum heat. Spread ¹⁄₁₆ inch of superfine sugar evenly over the surface of each dish. Place under the broiler, close to the flame, until the sugar caramelizes. (You can also use a mini blowtorch.) Serve immediately.

NOTE: Fresh passion-fruit juice is available at Dean and DeLuca.

MONTPELIER BUTTER

Adapted from Jeremiah Tower Cooks

YIELD: 1½ TO 2 CUPS

o o o

6 spinach leaves

Leaves from ½ bunch
watercress (1½ cups of
leaves)

2 tablespoons fresh flat-leaf
parsley leaves

2 tablespoons fresh chervil
leaves

2 tablespoons chopped
fresh chives

1 tablespoon fresh tarragon
leaves

2 shallots, chopped

2 cornichons, rinsed and
chopped

4 anchovy fillets

2 tablespoons capers

1 garlic clove, peeled

¼ teaspoon cayenne
pepper

3 hard-cooked egg yolks

2 large raw egg yolks

¼ pound unsalted butter, at
room temperature, cut
into 1-tablespoon
pieces

½ cup extra-virgin olive
oil

1 teaspoon white wine
vinegar

Salt

Freshly ground white
pepper

Blanch the spinach, watercress, herbs, and shallots in boiling water for 1 minute. Drain, refresh under cold water, and squeeze dry. Place the mixture in a food processor. Add the cornichons, anchovies, capers, garlic, cayenne, and salt and pepper to taste. Process to a smooth paste. Add the egg yolks, both cooked and raw, and the butter and process again until thoroughly mixed.

If the butter is still a little chunky (the sauce should be glossy and smooth as velvet), transfer the mixture to a blender and beat in the oil in a thin, steady stream while the blender is running. If the mixture is perfectly smooth in the food processor, transfer the butter to a bowl and whisk in the oil by hand. Beat in the vinegar and adjust the salt and pepper if necessary.

Epilogue

When I looked back over these essays I realized there was one extremely serious omission: not a single complete sentence was devoted to that revered Southern specialty—indeed, staple—pimento cheese. Though the *Times* did not, obviously, charge me with the mission of writing about Southern food, in most of the essays it just sort of turned out that way. But I must have drawn a subconscious line when it came to pimento cheese, otherwise known as "Southern pate" or "Carolina caviar." For all the current popularity of Southern food and Southern cookbooks, it is one of those things like yeast rolls or Marshall's biscuits (if I want them in New York, I hand carry them on the plane), or okra (it does not even rate a mention on New York's greenmarket harvest calendar) whose appeal stops at the Mason-Dixon line.

To me this is inexplicable. Pimento cheese is not only incredibly delicious, it stores and travels well, is cheaply made with what for most people are pantry staples, and it is versatile, which also means that it crosses class lines. It can be slathered on white bread for a quick sandwich eaten standing up in the kitchen, for example, but it is seen at least as often at cocktail parties stuffed into celery sticks, as a filling for dainty finger sandwiches, or piled neatly in a mound and served with crackers. My friend James Villas has been known to mix pimentos into cheese straw or cheese biscuit dough for pimento cheese straws and biscuits. Try the latter sliced open and buttered with a sliver of ham inside for a melding of two great classics—though I am firmly opposed to another such melding that results in pimento cheese deviled eggs. Still, there are few other things the stuff does not enhance.

The Varsity in Atlanta is famous for their hotdogs and hamburgers slathered with pimento cheese, and it was once featured on the cover of a Williams-Sonoma catalog atop miniburgers for the Fourth of July. The catalog inclusion marked a rare foray north, but it should be remembered that Chuck Williams, Williams-Sonoma's founder, hails from Memphis. In *Not Afraid of Flavor*, the indispensable cookbook by the chef/owners of Durham, North Carolina's Magnolia Grill, Ben and Karen Barker offer a recipe for "Okra Rellenos." In a particularly ingenious pairing, pimento cheese is stuffed into Talk 'O Texas pickled okra (by far the best brand and yet another thing I am forced to stuff into my luggage when I venture out of the region), lightly breaded with cornmeal, and fried. They are, quite simply, unbelievable.

Clearly, Yankees do not know what they are missing, but pretty much everybody else is clued in. In Texas, pimento cheese is most often made, naturally, with the addition of jalapeño peppers. In Georgia, sandwiches are sold at the concession stand of Augusta National, rather jarringly wrapped in green waxed pepper, and in the Augusta Junior League Cookbook, *Second Round: Teatime at the Masters*, a recipe for "zesty pimento cheese" includes the addition of prepared horseradish and mustard. At another Augusta establishment, Vera's Café, it is served with tomato and bacon on marbled rye.

The talented Scott Peacock reports that he not only eats pimento cheese every day, he serves it at his restaurant, Watershed, in Decatur, Georgia, several times a week: on sandwiches at lunch, as the chief ingredient of cheese toast at Sunday brunch, and in a little dish with crisp celery on the side as a dinner appetizer. Peacock, who correctly pronounces the stuff as "puhmenna cheese," is a purist, using white cheddar (because it is sharpest), orange cheddar (because "pimento cheese really needs to be orange"), mayonnaise, and chopped pimentos, along with black pepper and cayenne.

Reynolds Price, the North Carolina novelist and memoirist, calls pimento cheese "the peanut butter of his childhood," and his recipe matches that of his fellow Carolinian Villas almost word for word. Both men's essential instructions vary little from those of Peacock, except that each adds a squeeze of fresh lemon juice and Villas adds a dash of Worcestershire, while Price adds a clove of garlic and occasionally favors Tabasco over cayenne. All three are partial to either homemade mayonnaise or Duke's, which is made in Virginia and generally agreed upon as the best jarred mayo there is.

Villas's scant addition of lemon and Worcestershire is as much as he will mess with the basic combo. And he is especially vocal when it comes to such popular additions as dill or sweet pickle, onions, pecans, olives, curry powder, or cream cheese. "Since the marriage of cheddar and pimentos is blessed from on high and must therefore be treated with respect, never should any other ingredient be allowed to alter or nullify these primary flavors."

I take his point, but I have rarely come across homemade pimento cheese I didn't like (the storebought stuff, says Price, resembles "congealed chemicals"), and I also love that, like a lot of Southern standbys, ranging from fried chicken to pound cake, each cook can have his or her own way with it. Mississippi Delta–born

Craig Claiborne adds both scallions and garlic to his pimento cheese. I always look forward to festive outdoor events because I know that my friend Cameron Seward will be bringing it along, piled in a white porcelain bowl and usually accompanied by bagel crisps. Cameron is from Yazoo City, Mississippi, and by now the dish has become as much her signature as Claiborne's.

My friend Keith Meacham has perfected a recipe from her college roommate at Virginia, the secret of which is olive juice, which would likely make Villas scream, but he should try it. She served it on finger sandwiches at the luncheon she gave for my husband and me when we got married—along with ham biscuits and fried chicken, to complete my own personal holy trinity. It is so good that the two of us have been known to clean out a whole bowl in less than an hour. But my favorite by far—perhaps because it was the pimento cheese of my childhood—was created by Mary Bell Wright, the McGees' cook when we were growing up. She made it a lot and Bossy was smart enough to stand next to her plenty of times when she did. Though Mary Bell, sadly, is no longer with us, her superlative pimento cheese lives on.

Claiborne was the beneficiary of a food tester and cookbook editor, but I have tried to incorporate Keith's and Anne Ross's notes to me in their recipes because they are reflective of the way we all really cook. I usually find that when cooks tinker and taste, great things result from the process.

CRAIG CLAIBORNE'S
PIMENTO CHEESE SPREAD

YIELD: 8 TO 12 SERVINGS

. . .

½ pound mild yellow cheddar or longhorn cheese

½ pound white aged sharp cheddar cheese

1 can (7 ounces) pimentos

1 cup chopped scallions, including green parts

½ cup mayonnaise

2 teaspoons lemon juice

1 teaspoon finely minced garlic

2 tablespoons Worcestershire sauce

6 drops Tabasco sauce

½ teaspoon freshly ground black pepper

Use a meat grinder, if possible, to grate the cheese, using the cutter with large holes. Otherwise, use the coarse side of a cheese grater.

Put the grated cheese in a mixing bowl and add half the juice from the canned pimentos. Dice the drained pimentos and add them along with the scallions.

Combine the mayonnaise, lemon juice, and garlic and add to the cheese mixture. Add the Worcestershire, Tabasco, and pepper and blend well. Serve at room temperature as a spread for crisp crackers and raw vegetables or use as a sandwich spread.

NOTE: Unused pimento cheese may be tightly sealed and kept for several days in the refrigerator.

KEITH'S PIMENTO CHEESE SPREAD

YIELD: 12 SERVINGS

• • •

1 block Cracker Barrel extra-sharp white Vermont cheese,
    coarsely grated
1 block Cracker Barrel extra-sharp yellow cheese, grated
1 cup freshly grated aged Parmesan
1 teaspoon Dijon mustard
2 small jars chopped pimentos, drained
1 dash of juice from a jar of stuffed green cocktail olives
1 dash of fresh lemon juice
1 dash of Tabasco
1 dash of black pepper
1 cup Hellman's mayonnaise

Combine all ingredients with a fork or wooden spoon and refrigerate for at least three hours.

Taste. If it needs more bite, add more olive juice, Tabasco, or
pepper.

NOTE: Keith says, "Sometimes I use more pimentos, depending
on how much texture I want the thing to have." She also counsels
that "the cheaper the olives the better the juice," and to be careful
with it, as too much can make the recipe "watery," while not
enough means there won't be enough salt. As for the lemon juice,
she says it's there "because I add lemon to everything."

MARY BELL'S PIMENTO CHEESE

8 ounces sharp cheddar, coarsely grated
8 ounces mild cheddar, coarsely grated
⅛ of a white onion, finely grated
5 shakes of Lea & Perrins Worcestershire sauce
5 drops of Tabasco
⅛ cup sugar
1 large jar chopped pimentos, with juice
Mayonnaise, at least ¾ of a cup
1 small jar pimentos, drained (optional)

Mix all ingredients, except mayonnaise and the small jar of pimentos. Add mayonnaise until right consistency is reached.

NOTE: Bossy says the amount of mayonnaise added really depends on the amount of juice in the can with the pimentos, and that you just have to add it slowly and see what seems right. She also says that Mary Bell usually added the small drained can of pimentos at the end and "just barely swirled them in to make it look pretty."

HICKMANS

Brunswick County Library
109 W. Moore Street
Southport NC 28461

WITHDRAWN